From Hunter to Hunted

Other Books by Bernard Edwards

Masters Next to God
They Sank the Red Dragon
The Fighting Tramps
The Grey Widow-Maker
Blood and Bushido
SOS – Men against the Sea
Salvo!
Attack and Sink
Dönitz and the Wolf Packs
Return of the Coffin Ships
Beware Raiders!
The Road to Russia
The Quiet Heroes
The Twilight of the U-boats
Beware the Grey Widow-Maker
Death in the Doldrums
Japan's Blitzkrieg
War of the U-boats
Royal Navy versus the Slave Trade
The Cruel Sea Retold
War under the Red Ensign 1914–1918
The Wolf Packs Gather
Convoy Will Scatter
The Decoys
U-boats Beyond Biscay
Churchill's Thin Grey Line

From Hunter to Hunted

The U-Boat War in the Atlantic, 1939–1943

Bernard Edwards

Pen & Sword
MARITIME

First published in Great Britain in 2020 by
PEN & SWORD MARITIME
An imprint of
Pen & Sword Books Ltd
Yorkshire – Philadelphia

ISBN 978 1 52676 359 4

A CIP catalogue record for this book is available from the British Library.

Printed and bound in the UK
by TJ International Ltd, Padstow, Cornwall.

Pen & Sword Books Limited incorporates the imprints of Atlas, Archaeology,
Aviation, Discovery, Family History, Fiction, History, Maritime, Military,
Military Classics, Politics, Select, Transport, True Crime, Air World, Frontline
Publishing, Leo Cooper, Remember When, Seaforth Publishing, The Praetorian
Press, Wharncliffe Local History, Wharncliffe Transport, Wharncliffe True
Crime and White Owl.

For a complete list of Pen & Sword titles please contact

PEN & SWORD BOOKS LIMITED
47 Church Street, Barnsley, South Yorkshire, S70 2AS, England
E-mail: enquiries@pen-and-sword.co.uk
Website: www.pen-and-sword.co.uk

Or

PEN AND SWORD BOOKS
1950 Lawrence Rd, Havertown, PA 19083, USA
E-mail: Uspen-and-sword@casematepublishers.com
Website: www.penandswordbooks.com

'The focal war against England and the one possibility of bringing her to her knees lies in attacking sea communications in the Atlantic.'

Kommodore Karl Dönitz
Führer der Untersee-Boote
May 1939

*This book is dedicated to all those who gave
their lives to prove Dönitz wrong.*

Contents

Prologue

The Second World War opened with Britain's command of the sea unchallenged. As befitted an island nation holding sway over more than a fifth of the world, her navy was the biggest and best, standing in September 1939 at a massive fifteen battleships, six aircraft carriers, fifteen heavy cruisers, forty light cruisers, six anti-aircraft cruisers, 181 destroyers, fifty-nine submarines and forty-two minesweepers. Hitler's Kriegsmarine, on the other hand, was made up of only two battleships, three armoured cruisers, two heavy cruisers, six light cruisers, twenty-two destroyers, twenty motor torpedo boats and fifty-nine submarines. However, it must be said that much of the British fleet was of First World War vintage, while the German ships were all comparatively new. Nevertheless, no one considered the German Navy to be a credible threat to the sea lanes, least of all the men who manned Britain's merchant ships. They had supreme confidence in the Royal Navy to see them through.

It seems that memories were short, and the dreadful toll exacted by the Kaiser's U-boats in the 1914–1918 war had been forgotten. Few appeared to take notice of the new threat posed by the German U-boat arm, growing stronger by the day as her shipyards worked around the clock to swell the ranks of the undersea flotillas. In the opinion of Kommodore Karl Dönitz, the architect of Germany's plan to impose a total stranglehold on Britain's vital sea lanes, 'By our geographical position and inferiority to English sea power the U-boat is the means, above all the battle means of our Navy which can be committed to the decisive battle against English sea communications by itself with the greatest security.' Dönitz was aiming for a fleet of 300 U-boats.

After 1918, as stipulated by the Treaty of Versailles, the German Navy was reduced to six battleships of no more than 10,000 tons, six cruisers, twelve destroyers and twelve motor torpedo boats. The U-boat, which had created such havoc in the First World War, was no longer allowed, and for many years Berlin adhered to the letter of the Treaty. Following the dismantling of much of its heavy industry, and the crippling sanctions imposed by the victorious Allies, the Weimar Republic was more concerned with feeding its people and combating rampant inflation than rebuilding a navy which was apparently no longer required. By the time Hitler seized power in January 1933, stability had been achieved, and thoughts were turned to exacting revenge for the terrible humiliation Britain and her allies had inflicted on the Fatherland in 1918. Largely through the efforts of Karl Dönitz, clandestine yards were set up in Holland, parts were prefabricated in Austria, and by the time war threatened again, in the summer of 1939, Germany had acquired fifty-seven modern, ocean-going submarines. They were to be the spearhead of Hitler's Kriegsmarine.

On 19 August 1939, with war in Europe only weeks away, Dönitz despatched fourteen of his new Type VII and Type IX ocean-going boats from Wilhelmshaven out into the North Atlantic to sit astride Britain's sea lanes to the Americas. Six days later, fourteen of the smaller Type IIs entered the North Sea to take up similar strategic positions. Before a shot had been fired on land, Germany's Navy was ready to go to war.

Under the terms of the Prize Ordinance of 1936, to which Germany was a signatory, submarines were duty bound to surface and establish that a merchant ship was a legitimate target before opening fire on her. That being done, before sinking the ship the safety of her crew must be first ensured, and as the Prize Ordinance did not consider a ship's lifeboat to be a 'safe place', this should involve finding and stopping another ship to put them aboard. Failing that, the submarine was tasked with towing the ship's lifeboats to within sight of the nearest land. In a war situation this provision was clearly nonsensical, as it could put the attacking submarine in great danger. Nevertheless, in the early days of the war, U-boat commanders did their best to comply with the Ordinance.

Drawing on experience gained in the First World War, the arming of British merchant ships began some weeks before the commencement of hostilities in September 1939. The weapons supplied were largely 4-inch Mk VII, low-angle guns surplus to requirements in the Royal Navy which had been mothballed by the Admiralty in 1918. They were still usable, but ancient relics, which to comply with the Geneva Convention could only be mounted on the stern of a merchant ship, facing aft. As such, they were purely defensive guns, to be used when running away from an attacker.

As the war progressed, and some uncooperative British ship's captains began to use their guns to good effect, U-boat commanders surfacing to challenge often found themselves facing a hail of shells as their quarry turned tail and ran for the horizon. For the U-boats it was a situation fraught with danger, and it led to Dönitz issuing Standing Order No.154, which read:

> Rescue no one and take no one on board. Do not concern yourselves with the ship's boats. Weather conditions and the proximity of land are of no account. Care only for your own boat and strive to achieve the next success as soon as possible! We must be hard in this war. The enemy started the war in order to destroy us, therefore nothing else matters.

Following the circulation of Dönitz's Standing Order, the war in the North Atlantic underwent a dramatic change. The gloves were off, and the U-boats fought as they were intended to fight. No longer did they risk surfacing to put the cautionary shot across the bows and send a boarding party across to examine a ship's papers. They became the silent killers, operating at periscope depth, torpedoing indiscriminately. The Atlantic sea lanes became a bloodbath, littered with the wreckage of sunken ships and the pitiful flotsam of lifeboats and rafts carrying those lucky enough to survive a sinking. This situation prevailed until late 1943, with Britain and her faithful allies haemorrhaging ships and men to the U-boats at an ever increasing rate. The culmination of this indiscriminate slaughter came with the devastating attack on the two eastbound convoys SC 122 and HX 229 in March 1943 by a concentration of thirty-eight U-boats, resulting in the destruction of twenty-two loaded Allied ships. This was high water for the U-boats, but the tide was about to turn.

PART ONE

In the Beginning

CHAPTER ONE

Commence Hostilities

On 21 August 1939, thirteen days before the outbreak of the Second World War, Kommodore Karl Dönitz, C-in-C U-boats, sent the following report to his superiors in Berlin:

> The Atlantic boats are on their way to their positions. I am of the opinion that the convoy system will not come into full effect in the first days of the war. Even if the government were to order it at once, there would still be many single ships on the sea routes until it had got started. The important thing is to catch these ships at once.

One of Dönitz's Atlantic boats then taking up her allotted position was U-38, under the command of Kapitänleutnant Heinrich Liebe. She was some 80 miles due west of Lisbon, astride the well-trodden route taken by British merchantmen on their way to and from the far outposts of the Empire, outward deep-laden with the products of British industry, homeward with the spoils of colonialism. Until the starting gun for war was finally fired, Liebe was under orders to wait and observe these plump geese as they sailed by, unarmed, unescorted and unsuspecting. It was a frustrating exercise, but Liebe was warmed by the knowledge that when the time came, a quick shot across the bows would be enough to send their crews running for the boats.

U-38, one of a series of eight large ocean-going boats built in 1938 primarily for long-range operations, displaced 1,016 tons on the surface and had a top speed of 18.2 knots. She was armed with six torpedo tubes, four in the bows and two aft, and carried sixteen extra torpedoes, ten of which were in external containers. Her secondary armament consisted of a 105mm deck gun and two smaller AA guns. As yet untried in battle, she had huge potential, as did her commander, 31-year-old Heinrich Liebe, a long-serving naval officer. He had spent some years in the battleship *Schleswig-Holstein* before transferring to the newly-formed U-boat arm in 1935 with the rank of Oberleutnant zur See. He then spent two years in command of the small coastal boat U-2, before commissioning U-38 when she was completed in 1938.

At 1246 Central European Time on 3 September 1939 Berlin sent the following signal to all U-boats:

OPEN HOSTILITIES AGAINST ENGLAND IMMEDIATELY.
DO NOT WAIT TO BE ATTACKED FIRST.

The British steamer *Manaar* was ten hours out of Liverpool and passing Tuskar Rock in the St George's Channel, when she received news that Britain was at war with Germany. The news came as no great surprise to Captain Campbell Shaw and his crew, for they had been well briefed prior to sailing. Code books in weighted bags had been put aboard, and a gun had been mounted aft on the poop. The gun, a Mk V 12-pounder, was a simple 3-inch calibre weapon, its like having been in use with the Royal Navy since the Boer War of 1899, although the gun in question was not quite so ancient. Firing over open sights, it could be handled by a small crew with a basic knowledge of gunnery. This was just as well, since the only man on board with any gunnery training was the *Manaar's* Second Officer, who had attended a two-day course at HMS *Eaglet* while in Liverpool. This officer was tasked with forming and training a gun's crew from his fellow officers during the outward passage.

The 7,242-ton *Manaar*, built in 1917 and owned by the long established shipping company T. & J. Brocklebank, was a cargo liner employed mainly between British and Indian ports. She carried a total complement of seventy, comprising fifteen European officers and petty officers, and fifty-five Indian ratings, the customary manning for ships in that trade. Coal-fired, she was powered by two geared steam turbines driving a single shaft, giving her a service speed of 12 knots. On her current voyage she was bound for Calcutta and Rangoon with a general cargo that included a substantial amount of agricultural machinery and government stores.

The state of war in the North Atlantic, as Captain Shaw understood it, was that the small number of German U-boats then at sea were concentrated in the western approaches to the British Isles, so that once the *Manaar* was south of Ushant she was unlikely to be troubled. Accordingly, he had decided to follow the customary route to the Mediterranean, passing 20 miles off Ushant and

Cape Finisterre, then parallel to the coasts of Spain and Portugal, rounding Cape St Vincent at about 10 miles, before entering the Straits of Gibraltar.

As Captain Shaw had rightly anticipated, the *Manaar* steamed south without incident, encountering only the normal stream of up and down traffic, exactly as she would have done before war was declared. Shortly after sunrise on the 5th, she was within sight of the rocky peninsula of Finisterre and, uncertain of the neutrality of Spain and Portugal, Shaw edged away from the coast to gain some sea room. There had still been no sighting of the enemy.

Unknown to Captain Shaw, just out of sight over the horizon some miles to the south, U-38 was already at work. Liebe had stopped and boarded the French steamer *Pluvoise*, an action which at that time was contrary to orders. Although the French had declared war on Germany within hours of the British declaration, Berlin was still not sure that the French had any serious intent, and instructions had been issued for the U-boats to avoid all contact with French vessels. Bearing this in mind, Liebe detained the *Pluvoise* only long enough to examine her papers, then sent her on her way.

It may be that stopping the French ship had been an excusable lapse on Liebe's part, but releasing her only compounded the error. As soon as U-38 was out of sight, the *Pluvoise* had broadcast a warning to all ships that a U-boat was active in the area. This message was intercepted by Berlin and resulted in Heinrich Liebe receiving a severe reprimand.

Also listening to the *Pluvoise*'s submarine alert was the *Manaar*'s wireless operator, James Gordon Melville Turner. All British merchant ships would soon be required to carry three operators keeping watch around the clock, but for the time being Turner was on his own. His working day consisted of ten hours in two-hour watches from dawn to dusk, and it was only by chance that he was on watch when the *Pluvoise* sent out her warning. He immediately passed the message to Captain Shaw, who was quick to take action, posting extra lookouts, adopting a zig-zag course and darkening ship at night. The 12-pounder, sitting forlorn on the *Manaar*'s poop, he was inclined to ignore, as there had not yet been time to train up a gun's crew.

Summer had not yet run its full course in the northern hemisphere, and the *Manaar* enjoyed favourable weather in the opening days of her voyage. Once south of Finisterre she encountered the Portuguese trades in the form of a moderate following wind that ruffled the sea with a scattering of white horses and from time to time enveloped the bridge in acrid-smelling funnel smoke. In turn, the helping hand of the trades gave her an extra half knot to speed her on her way.

When dawn broke on 6 September, after another quiet night, star sights showed the *Manaar* to be 70 miles west of Lisbon. Captain Shaw was already on the bridge and contemplating the empty horizon with growing confidence. The indications were that they had eluded the clutches of Hitler's U-boats. Then U-38 surfaced on the port bow.

Since his unfortunate run-in with the French steamer *Pluvoise*, Heinrich Liebe had vowed to be more cautious in his approach to enemy shipping. Throughout the previous night he had been shadowing the *Manaar* on the surface, uncertain of her nationality, and submerging at first light. He had then monitored her movements through his periscope, and it was not until he saw the Red Ensign being raised at her stern that he surfaced.

Liebe was first out of the conning tower hatch as U-38 broke the surface, and he lost no time in running his binoculars over the British ship. The 12-pounder on her poop immediately caught his attention, and when he saw movement near the gun he sent his gun's crew forward with orders to put a shot across her bows.

On the bridge of the *Manaar* Captain Shaw and Chief Officer Evans, shocked by the sudden appearance of the U-boat, had in turn snatched up their binoculars. Their hopes that she was a Royal Navy submarine keeping a watchful eye on them were dashed when the swastika was run up at her stern and a puff of white smoke appeared forward of her conning tower. The 105mm shell whistled across the *Manaar*'s bows to explode in the water close to starboard. The war had caught up with her.

The situation being clear, Captain Shaw ordered the helm hard to starboard, rang for full emergency speed and blew a series of short blasts on the steam whistle for action stations, all in quick succession. Then, having brought the U-boat astern, he steadied the *Manaar* on a northerly course and informed the engine room of the situation, calling for every possible revolution they could coax out of their ageing machinery. In the dim reaches of her stokehold the *Manaar*'s furnace doors clanged open, and the wiry

Indian firemen hurled shovel after shovel of best Welsh into the roaring fires. The *Manaar* settled her stern deeper in the water, and her bow wave rose as she strained every rivet to escape from her attacker. Shaw then gave orders for the 12-pounder to be manned and sent the standby quartermaster to call the Radio Officer.

Radio Officer Gordon Turner's reactions are on record:

> I was awakened early on the morning of the 6th September by a succession of short blasts on the steam whistle. I jumped out of bed, and went to the cabin door, looked out, and Quartermaster Jones who was passing at the time told me that a submarine was on the surface. I slipped on a dressing gown and went up to the Radio Room which is abaft the chartroom on the bridge. I then came out of the wireless room on to the bridge to let the Master see that I was on watch. I returned to the radio room and prepared the submarine message for transmission. Gun firing started shortly after I went into the room.

As soon as the U-boat had been brought astern, the *Manaar*'s 12-pounder opened fire, but the shot fell well short. The maximum range of the Mk V 12-pounder was listed as 6½ miles, but this gun was of First World War vintage, and the rifling of its barrel was probably worn smooth. The range was obviously far too great, and rather than waste ammunition, Captain Shaw ordered the Second Officer to cease fire.

Having in mind the limitation of the Prize Regulations, Heinrich Liebe had intended to await the reaction to his shot across the bows of the *Manaar*, but the precipitate firing of the British ship's 12-pounder provided him with the excuse to launch an attack in self-defence. He therefore ordered his gun's crew to sink his armed opponent.

U-38 opened fire in earnest, and a rain of shot descended on the British ship, blowing away the port side of her bridge house. Within minutes she had been hit six times, her wireless aerial was brought down and a number of small fires had been started.

Radio Officer Turner was unaware that his aerial had been shot away:

> After a certain number of shots had been fired, the Captain opened a trap between the chartroom and the wireless

room and instructed me to broadcast the submarine signal, and at the same time to give the ship's position.

I started up the main transmitter and commenced sending the message. At the same time I noticed that the aerial and the meter were not registering. All the other indications were satisfactory, so I concluded there was something wrong with the aerial circuit. I investigated that and could not find any trouble, so I had another effort at getting the message away, but it was no good. I switched over to the emergency, which is an entirely separate transmitter, except that it uses the same aerial. During this time the ship was under constant gunfire.

U-38's gunners had found the range, and their shells were hitting home with frightening regularity. Captain Shaw reluctantly came to the conclusion that escape was impossible and that he must surrender to save the lives of his crew. He rang the engines to stop, and as the *Manaar* lost way through the water he sent Chief Officer Evans below to organize the lowering of the lifeboats. The ensign was then lowered to indicate surrender.

The *Manaar* was now at Liebe's mercy, but instead of ceasing fire, as Shaw had expected, he ordered his gunners to switch from H.E. to shrapnel. Surprised and annoyed that this rather ancient-looking merchantman had had the audacity to return his fire, Liebe seemed determined to teach her a lesson. The *Manaar*'s scuppers ran red with the blood of men cut down as they ran for the boats.

U-38 was slowly but surely overtaking the British ship and was now close on her port beam, her shells hitting home relentlessly. Under the circumstances, it would not have been surprising if discipline had gone to the winds and panic had broken out amongst the *Manaar*'s crew, but Captain Shaw and his officers held the line. To accommodate her complement of seventy, the *Manaar* carried six lifeboats in all, four large boats on the boat deck and two smaller ones alongside the bridge. The four large boats were lowered safely, and the survivors boarded, but before leaving the ship Captain Shaw searched the decks and accommodation but could find no one else alive. Unfortunately, in the heat of the moment, Radio Officer Turner was forgotten, and the boats pulled away without him.

Thirty-two-year-old Gordon Turner was a fastidious individual; he was also a brave man, and while the others were abandoning ship he had stayed at his key attempting to get away a distress signal. Only when he discovered that his wireless aerial had been shot away did he finally give up. He then went to report to the bridge, but found it deserted. He searched around but found no one. Then he discovered that the lifeboats were in the water and pulling away from the ship. He had been left behind.

Alone, and on a ship under fire and liable to be sunk at any moment, Turner looked around for a means of escape. His only hope seemed to be to launch one of the small lifeboats still secured in their davits alongside the bridge. He first went below to his cabin to collect his lifejacket. When he was about to return to the bridge, he discovered that he was not alone after all. Two Lascar firemen, both of whom were wounded, had also been left behind. He called on them to help him lower one of the bridge boats, but one was too badly injured to be of any use, and the other man was not interested.

Captain Shaw, meanwhile, had discovered that his radio officer was still on board the ship and was making every effort to bring his boat back alongside. The boat was no more than half a mile from the ship, but its engine had broken down, and with the wind and sea against them the heavy wooden craft was proving almost impossible to row.

Had Gordon Turner been alone, he would have gone over the side and attempted to swim towards the boat, but he now had two injured men on his hands and as a ship's officer he was responsible for them. To save them, and himself, he had somehow to get one of the bridge boats into the water. Both boats were swung out ready for lowering, but still bowsed in to the ship by their belly bands. Under normal circumstances, at least two men would have been required to lower such a boat, one tending each fall. Turner tried to persuade the less injured fireman to help, but the man was resigned to his fate and flatly refused to move. In desperation, Turner cleared away the starboard boat, but as he had feared, his attempt to lower it alone ended in disaster. One of the falls ran away, and the boat nose-dived into the sea, drifting away waterlogged. Turner later wrote in his report:

I then went to the port side, for there was one more boat. This boat was still made fast with the belly strap. I was in the act of slackening that off when I heard cries from the native I had seen from the bridge previously. I called him to come forward to the boat. He was in a sitting position, and apparently could only shuffle about, so I went aft and carried him off the boat deck and took him to the lifeboat and placed him inside. His left leg was apparently very seriously wounded. The trouser leg was saturated with blood.

I then started to slacken off the belly strap, and was bending down on that job when there was an explosion which threw me flat on my stomach, and I felt debris coming down on my back.

Heinrich Liebe's patience had finally run out. Failing to sink the British ship by gunfire, and now fearing for the safety of his boat, he had dived to periscope depth and fired a torpedo, hoping to finish what was rapidly becoming a farce. The torpedo hit the *Manaar* squarely amidships, directly below her bridge. With the sea pouring in to her breached hull, she began to settle bodily.

When he had recovered from the shock of the explosion, Radio Officer Turner's first reaction was to reach for his lifejacket, which had been on the deck beside him. It was no longer there, blown over the side along with the lifeboat and the injured man inside. All that remained were a few scraps of smoking wreckage.

Turner's predicament had been witnessed by Captain Shaw, prompting him to redouble his efforts to return to the ship. His boat's crew responded well, bending their backs to the oars with a will. Aboard the *Manaar*, Turner had collected the remaining fireman, and both men had gone forward onto the foc'sle head ready to jump. Gordon Turner continues the narrative:

I searched around under the foc'sle head and found a rope that I lowered over the side of the starboard bow. As I had no lifebelt and the sea was rather choppy and the nearest lifeboat was now some distance away, I looked around for some form of raft, and the best I could do was two 'NO SMOKING' notices about 2ft long. I lowered them over the side, and then noticed that the starboard lifeboat was drifting full of water a little short distance out. I immediately went down the rope, which I kept hold of, and swam out to the boat, climbed on board, and pulled it back alongside the short distance to the ship, and the lascar came down the rope into the boat. I then found that the lifeboat was made fast by the painter on board the ship. I searched in the boat and found an axe, hacked the painter through, and the boat drifted off. We both got an oar each out, and pulled the lifeboat in the direction of the Master's boat. With the help of the drift and our own pulling, the lifeboat was then picked up by the Master's boat, which pulled across towards us.

Shortly after Radio Officer Turner and the injured fireman transferred to Captain Shaw's lifeboat, Heinrich Liebe delivered the coup de grâce to the *Manaar* with two torpedoes fired singly. After the second torpedo slammed home into the doomed ship's hull, she broke in two and sank. Just over two hours had elapsed since Shaw and Evans had first sighted the U-boat. During this time, U-38 had fired over twenty rounds of 105mm ammunition and three torpedoes. Heinrich Liebe's first conquest of the war had cost him dear. As for the *Manaar*, she had earned the distinction of being the first British merchantman to return the fire of a German U-boat in the war, but this had been at a heavy price; in addition to the loss of the ship and her cargo, seven men had lost their lives, all of them Lascar seamen who were innocent participants in the conflict.

When she sank, the *Manaar* was about 65 miles west-north-west of Cape Roca, and her four lifeboats set course due west for the land. Captain Campbell Shaw and twenty-nine of his crew were picked up within sight of Cape Roca by the Dutch steamer *Mars*, sixteen others were found by the Portuguese passenger liner *Carvalho Aruajo*, while the Italian steamer *Castelbianco* rescued the remaining seventeen. All were landed in Lisbon.

Undoubtedly the hero of the hour was Radio Officer Gordon Turner, and he was duly rewarded for his brave conduct. The following announcement appeared in the *London Gazette* on 13 October 1939:

The King has been graciously pleased to approve the award of the Medal of the Civil Division of the Most Excellent Order of the British Empire for Gallantry to the undermentioned:

James Gordon Melville Turner, Radio Officer
s.s. Manaar (Messrs T & J Brocklebank)

When the S.S. Manaar was attacked by an enemy submarine there was no summons to stop. About ten shots were
fired before the ship was abandoned after twenty or thirty
minutes. Three shells were fired, one of which took away
the fore part of the wheelhouse and probably the wireless
aerial. Rapid shrapnel followed. Some of the men in the
boats were injured by gunfire.

The Radio Officer was inadvertently left behind in the
ship with two members of the native crew, one severely
wounded and the other injured. His shipmates called him
to come down and join them in the Master's boat, but he
refused to leave the ship until the other two members of
the crew could be rescued. He tried to lower a lifeboat,
but the falls jammed and then suddenly ran out, so that
the boat crashed into the water and filled. He carried the
severely wounded Lascar to another boat, and was about
to lower it when the boat was blown to pieces, with the
wounded man inside. He then swam out to the waterlogged boat and pulled her alongside. The injured Lascar
then went down the rope into the boat, which was cut
adrift, and joined the Master's boat. All this was done
under fire.

After a short spell of survivor's leave, Gordon Turner returned
to sea with T. & J. Brocklebank, but he was again torpedoed and
found himself in a lifeboat. This time the odds were stacked
too heavily against him. He lost a leg in the sinking, and spent
the rest of the war in a German prisoner of war camp. After the
war, having had his fill of the sea, he came ashore and moved
inland, buying a smallholding in Kent. He married in 1950 at the
age of forty-three, and had two children. After the birth of his
second child he found he was not making enough money out of
the smallholding to sustain his family, and he took a job in a car
factory in Luton, working nights for the extra money he needed.
Each weekend, he travelled home by train to be with his family.

On Sunday, 5 November 1967, as a result of strike action in the
factory, Turner was asked to return early to help keep production
running. He caught the train to Charing Cross, and at 9.16 pm,
when passing through Hither Green, near Lewisham, it crashed,
killing fifty-three people, among them Gordon Turner. Once again,

Turner had put duty before self, and this time it had cost him his life.

When, on the morning of 6 September 1939, U-38 attempted to stop the *Manaar* with a shot across her bows, Heinrich Liebe was adhering strictly to the Prize Ordinance of 1935 and the London Submarine Agreement of 1936, both of which Germany was signatory to. These treaties, in effect, stipulated that a submarine was permitted to stop and search any merchant ship suspected to be of the enemy's flag or carrying cargo for the enemy. If this was found to be so, then the submarine was justified in sinking that ship, but not before she had seen to the safety of her passengers and crew. In an all-out conflict such as the Second World War, when there was so much at stake on either side, this may seem somewhat naive, if not downright silly.

It seems likely that Heinrich Liebe was thinking along these lines when he challenged the *Manaar*, but when the British ship returned his fire, albeit with only one round from her 12-pounder, the Kapitänleutnant took exception and hurled the rule book over the side. He poured shell after shell into the *Manaar*, although it must then have been clearly evident that she had surrendered and her crew were taking to the boats. As a result of this vindictive attack, seven men died unnecessarily, and Liebe's reaction was an indication of the way the war at sea was to be conducted in the future. Less than two months were to pass before Dönitz issued Standing Order No. 154, which read:

> Rescue no one and take no one on board. Do not concern yourselves with the ship's boats. Weather conditions and the proximity of land are of no account. Care only for your own boat and strive to achieve the next success as soon as possible: we must be hard in this war. The enemy started the war in order to destroy us, therefore nothing else matters.

The words of the Führer der Unterseeboote heralded a dramatic change in the way the war between the U-boats and Allied merchant ships would be fought, but in the meantime the majority of U-boat commanders were determined to pay at least lip service to the Prize Ordinance.

CHAPTER TWO

One of Ropner's

Setting out from Kiel on 19 August 1939 with Dönitz's pathfinder flotilla of fifteen was the Type VIIB U-boat U-48 which, unknown to those then sailing in her, was embarking on a two-year-long career during which she would become the most successful submarine ever to fly the flag of Hitler's Kriegsmarine.

Entering the North Sea via the Skagerrak, U-48 rounded the north of Scotland and moved undetected into the Western Approaches. There she had orders to await the outcome of the politicians' last minute efforts to avoid another world war.

In command of U-48 was 30-year-old Kapitänleutnant Herbert Schultze, an experienced officer who had joined the then Reichsmarine in April 1930. He served first in the light cruisers *Leipzig* and *Karlsruhe*, before transferring to the U-boat arm in May 1937. Eight months later, after extensive training, he took command of the small coastal submarine U-2 and remained with her for the next fifteen months, before commissioning the ocean-going boat U-48 in April 1939.

Shortly before noon on 5 September 1939, two days after Great Britain's momentous decision to challenge the might of Hitler's Third Reich, U-48 had her first meeting with the enemy.

The 4,853-ton *Royal Sceptre,* sailing under the command of Captain James Gair, was 450 miles south-west of Land's End and nearing the end of a 6,000-mile voyage from Rosario, Argentina with a full cargo of wheat and maize. She was unescorted and unarmed, making her an easy target for Herbert Schultze's first shot fired in anger.

Schultze opened the attack with his 88mm deck gun, putting a warning shot across the *Royal Sceptre*'s bows. Captain Gair, understandably annoyed at this unwarranted attempt to interrupt what had otherwise been an untroubled voyage, immediately turned under full helm and presented his stern to the enemy submarine. He rang for emergency full speed, ordering his chief engineer to screw the boiler safety valves down, and the *Royal Sceptre* fled for the horizon at a speed she had never before achieved. It was a brave try, but doomed to end in failure.

Although only two years old, the *Royal Sceptre*, like all British tramps of the day, was built for economy rather than speed. The best her engineers could produce was a reluctant 12 knots, while U-48's twin diesels produced 16 knots with ease. It was Herbert Schultze's intention to overtake the *Royal Sceptre* and force her to surrender without another shot being fired, but the British ship sealed her own fate by using her radio to send an SOS. U-48's position was thus given away, and Schultze opened fire in earnest. Gair refused to surrender, and the chase went on for more than an hour and a half, during which time the *Royal Sceptre* was reduced to a burning hulk, Captain James Gair was killed on his bridge and nine others were wounded. Schultze delivered the coup de grâce with a torpedo, but then showed a more humane side by calling in another British merchantman to pick up the *Royal Sceptre*'s survivors.

Three days later, having moved deeper into the Atlantic, U-48 came across another British tramp, the 5,055-ton Cardiff-owned *Winkleigh*, commanded by Captain Thomas Georgeson. Bound from Vancouver to Manchester with a cargo of grain and timber, the *Winkleigh* was nearing the end of a long and arduous passage via the Panama Canal and proved to be an easy conquest for Herbert Schultze. She was unarmed and lacked the speed to escape. Not unwisely, Captain Georgeson chose to stop and haul down his flag when Schultze fired a warning shot, but not before an SOS had been sent out. After allowing the *Winkleigh*'s crew to take to their boats, Schultze sank the ship with a single torpedo, thus consigning another valuable cargo to the bottom of the ocean. Ironically, Captain Georgeson and his crew of thirty-six, who had been so near to the end of their voyage, were later picked up by the westbound Dutch passenger liner *Statendam* and carried back across the Atlantic to be landed in New York.

Schultze was now running short of fuel and torpedoes and, aware that his position had been given away by the two ships he had sunk, he decided it was time for U-48 to return home. The only way into Kiel was round the top of Scotland, and he set course to the north.

Two hundred and forty miles west-north-west of Cape Wrath, the British steamer *Firby* was taking full advantage of the fair weather. It being late summer, the North Atlantic was at its best; high pressure reigned, bringing clear blue skies and light winds, and the sea was no more than a gentle chop. The *Firby's* sturdy triple-expansion engine thumped away merrily, and a long streamer of black smoke trailed back from her tall funnel as she reeled off the miles. Unescorted and unarmed, she was to all outward appearances totally oblivious to the full-scale war that had broken out in Europe only days before. Her only concession to hostilities was an overall coat of Admiralty grey, hastily applied before she left dry dock in North Shields three days earlier.

Owned by the Ropner Steamship Company of West Hartlepool, the 4,869-ton *Firby* was a typical north-east coast tramp. Straight of stem, with a box-shaped hull, she was a prodigious cargo carrier, built with maximum of economy of operation in mind. Her 439 nominal horse power steam engine, powered by three Scotch boilers, offered reliability rather than speed, and at a steady 9 knots she was reckoned to be 'doing nicely'.

The *Firby* carried a crew of thirty-four, who were housed in the most basic of accommodation: navigating officers amidships, engineers further aft above their engine room, sailors and firemen in a foc'sle right aft. The food prepared in her small galley was said to be adequate and no more. There were certainly no frills to the *Firby*, and the men who manned her were to match. Under the command of 37-year-old Captain Thomas Prince, they worked hard and, whenever the opportunity arose, played hard, too. Faced by danger, they never failed to rise to the challenge.

The Ropner Steamship Company, founded in 1874 by the German-born Victorian entrepreneur Robert Ropner, was in the 1930s a major player in British shipping, being one of the world's largest general cargo carriers. In essence, its ships were tramps, ready to go anywhere and carry any cargo, but Ropner's main trade was in coal out from the Bristol Channel and grain home from Canada. The freight on these bulk cargoes was low, but they kept Ropner's ships in employment, even during the years of the Great Depression.

On the outbreak of war in 1939, all British merchant ships came under the direction of the Ministry of War Transport, and although they were as far as possible allowed to continue in their accustomed trade, they were liable to be used as required by the Ministry. In the case of the *Firby*, instead of proceeding to the

Bristol Channel to load coal, she had been ordered to sail directly to Port Churchill, Canada in ballast and there to take on her usual cargo of grain. In anticipation of a blockade by Germany, the granaries of Britain were being stocked up.

The *Firby* set sail from the Tyne on the morning of Friday, 8 September – not Friday the Thirteenth, perhaps, but the nearest thing to it. Seamen being by the nature of their calling profoundly superstitious, there were mutterings in the *Firby*'s foc'sle, and even Captain Prince would have preferred to wait until after midnight, but the weather clock was ticking.

Port Churchill, the *Firby*'s allotted loading port, described by one cynic as 'a windy, desolate icebog on the western shore of Canada's Hudson Bay', lies in latitude 58° 43'N, and has a sub-arctic climate. Its winters are bitterly cold and long drawn-out, while summer is short and cool. Hudson Bay freezes over in the winter and is only open to shipping from July to late October. Even in the so-called summer, the strait leading in to the bay is a navigator's nightmare, being plagued by fog and subject to magnetic influences that can set a ship's compass needle spinning. As soon as he had dropped his pilot at the mouth of the Tyne, Captain Prince called his Chief Engineer to the bridge and explained the situation. Their ship would never aspire to win the Blue Riband, but a fast passage was imperative.

Following the route prescribed by the Admiralty, the *Firby* made her way up the North Sea and rounded the north of Scotland via the Pentland Firth, being abeam of the lighthouse on Cape Wrath by about 2300 on the 9th. It was a fine, clear night, with little in the way of wind, and with the barometer standing high and steady, there seemed every possibility of an untroubled crossing.

The *Firby* was clear of the Outer Hebrides by 0300 on the 10th, and Captain Prince decided to go below to snatch a few hours' sleep; but before he could do so, a signal lamp stabbed the darkness challenging the British tramp to identify herself. Her challenger turned out to be a light cruiser of the Northern Patrol, which had been set up to intercept enemy merchant ships attempting to return to Germany by the northern route and to prevent German commerce raiders breaking out into the Atlantic. The *Firby* was ordered to reverse course and head east again and, accompanied by the cruiser, she retraced her steps. She was taken into sheltered waters off the north of Scotland and boarded by the Royal Navy. Her papers were examined, the ship searched, and it having been established that she was indeed a British merchantman going about her lawful business, she was allowed to continue her voyage.

The sun was well up when the *Firby* steamed past Cape Wrath for the second time and out into the open Atlantic. Tom Prince, frustrated and anxious to make up for lost time, rang for full speed, and by noon on the 11th the *Firby* was curtseying to the long Atlantic swells as she pushed on to the west. Before sailing from the Tyne three days earlier, Prince had been assured by the Navy that he had little to fear from the U-boats, as they were all congregating in the Western and South-Western Approaches. However, he was no stranger to war. Son of an Army captain, he had first gone to sea as a young apprentice in 1917, when the First World War, in which two of his brothers were killed in the trenches, was at its height, and he had not forgotten the lessons learned then. In the absence of any defensive armament – other than the .38 revolver locked in his safe – he had swung his lifeboats out ready for lowering and posted extra lookouts. He could do no more.

Lunch over, Captain Prince was back on the bridge scanning the horizon ahead, which was unsullied, except for the odd seabird. Slowly, he relaxed, unaware that he was being watched.

Half a mile astern of the *Firby*, on her port quarter, Herbert Schultze was at periscope depth and examining the British ship closely. Following the sinking of the *Winkleigh* three days earlier, U-48 had travelled north on the surface without sighting a single ship, enemy or otherwise. Now, finding the *Firby* alone on an empty ocean, the German commander was suspicious. As far as he could make out, she was unarmed, but mindful that the British had in the First World War used Q-ships, Navy-manned merchantmen with guns hidden behind shutters, he was suspicious. Schultze looked long and hard before he gave the order to surface.

A shout from the masthead lookout alerted Captain Prince to the conning tower of U-48 emerging from the sea. He focussed his binoculars and saw men appear on her casings and run for the forward mounted gun. There was no challenge, no warning from the submarine, but her intent was obvious. Without waiting to investigate, Prince gave a double ring on the engine room telegraph and brought his attacker right astern. The *Firby*'s engine note quickened, and she surged forward. At that, Schultze opened fire with his 88mm. Captain Prince wrote in his report:

> I zig-zagged all the time but each shell, including the first shell, hit us. He put one through the firemens' bathroom, one through No.2 hold, one through my room, one through the funnel, one carried away the wireless downlead and the other one hit the after-deck. Two men were wounded by that shot. We had four men wounded in all by the shooting.

It was obvious to Prince that he was in a fight he had no hope of winning, and with six of his crew lying wounded and his ship being slowly being destroyed by the enemy submarine's accurate shooting, he had no choice but to surrender. He rang the engines to stop, lowered his ensign and ordered his crew to abandon ship. When Schultz saw the *Firby*'s lifeboats being lowered, he had the decency to cease fire, allowing her crew, including their wounded, to get clear of their doomed ship. Captain Prince wrote:

> The submarine hailed my boat alongside. He asked for the Captain of the ship and then ordered me to come on board and bring my papers. They wanted any secret documents or papers I had. I told him that I had none because I had already destroyed them. I had all the books together in an unweighted bag and I myself saw them sink; and the papers I tore into small pieces. I told him that I had no secret papers as we were the first ship to leave without convoy and the Admiralty did not think it necessary for me to have any secret orders. He asked me what I was doing in the position I was in. I told him I always made that route when bound for Port Churchill. He asked me where Port Churchill was, and when I told him that it was Hudson Bay he said, 'All right', as I told him I always sighted Greenland on my passage. He took the ship's Articles as a souvenir. He then asked me to have a drink with him, so we both had a tumbler full of whisky. He told me he would send an SOS out to Churchill and wished me the best of luck and hoped we would meet again after the war was over. He gave me four rolls of bandages and six loaves of bread for the wounded. He called the boat back

alongside. He let me go and gave me the course to steer. We went off in the lifeboats, I called the other lifeboats alongside and, after I left the submarine, he torpedoed the ship and he remained on the surface until the ship was sunk and then submerged heading for the southward. I called the other boats alongside and I told them to keep together and when mine approached we laid to with the sea anchor out, about 9 pm. The other lifeboat foundered so I had to take the crew from that lifeboat into mine. We laid to sea anchor till about 2.45 or 3 in the morning . . .

Of his visit to U-48, Captain Prince had this to say:

The officer who interviewed me was thin-faced and had a long narrow face. He was unshaven, with about three weeks' growth, and dark. His build was slight but he would be about 5' 10" in height. His English was not very fluent but rather broken and he had a marked guttural accent. He was very polite and in no way bullied me, gave me a cigarette and, as I have said, a drink. This officer was undoubtedly the commander, judging from the way in which he gave orders to everyone else. When I last saw him, he was standing in the conning tower with his hand to his forehead in salute. He was wearing a big reefer coat with an old uniform cap of blue colour. There was a badge on this cap, but I did not see what it was. The Commander asked me how many ships the U-boats had sunk and I said, 'Only five up to now', and he said, 'And this one the sixth?', and I said, 'Yes', and he said, 'Well, that is not many, is it?'

The Second-in-Command behaved in a very hostile and unpleasant fashion. When the Commander gave me a cigarette, I offered him one in return and at the same time offered one to the other officer, who refused to take it and he looked at me the whole time I was in the U-boat as though he would like to behave in a very different manner from the Commander. The second officer was older distinctly than the Commander and he had a beard which I describe as a 'von Tirpitz type'. He was shorter – only about 5' 6" in height. He was wearing a uniform coat with a badge which I could not read, but no rings. It was a pretty old coat. The clothing of the crew was quite nondescript and there was nothing in the nature of uniform worn.

When Prince returned to his lifeboat he was astonished to find that, while he had been aboard the U-boat, Schultze's men had dressed and bandaged the wounds of his injured crew members.

True to his word, once clear of the area, Herbert Schultze sent the following radio message to Winston Churchill, then First Lord of the Admiralty:

cq - cq – cq – transmit to Mr. Churchill. I have sunk the British steamer 'Firby'. Posit. 59.40 North and 13.50 West. Save the crew, if you please.

Schultze's message was picked up by the American merchant ship *Scanpenn*, which in turn relayed it to the Admiralty at Rosyth. Thirteen hours later, Captain Tom Prince and his crew of thirty-three were picked up by the destroyer HMS *Fearless* and landed at Scapa Flow.

On 11 September Dönitz made the following entry in his War Diary:

Radio intelligence report of the sinking of the S.S. Firby (4683 BRT) in square 1366 AM west of the Faroes. This success should have a very strong effect, as so far U-boats have not appeared in this area. Radio intelligence reports of convoys are coming in in increasing numbers. The rendezvous in the Bristol Channel are still being transmitted to the boats. Otherwise there is no clear picture.

Having evaded the Northern Patrol, U-48 rounded the north coast of Scotland and returned to Kiel at the end of a successful first war patrol lasting twenty-nine days, during which she had sunk three ships totalling 14,777 gross tons. Thus Herbert Schultze had inflicted a heavy loss on British shipping without losing a single man killed. He had also shown the face of humanity, if only briefly.

Captain Tom Prince was back at sea within weeks of losing the *Firby*, and in December of that same year was in command of Ropner's 4,876-ton *Otterpool*, another ageing tramp built in the same West Hartlepool yard and in the same year as the *Firby*.

The war now being in its third month, the *Otterpool* had been given the means to hit back at the enemy, a 4-inch anti-submarine gun and a 12-pounder for use against aircraft. Both guns were of First World War vintage, mothballed in an Admiralty dock-yard for twenty-odd years, and in accordance with the Geneva Convention were both mounted right aft for use in defence only. With them had come a team of two DEMS gunners, who main-tained the guns and would be backed up by the ship's crew when it came to action.

That action came soon after the *Otterpool*'s guns had been fitted. She was off the east coast of Scotland, in the vicinity of the Firth of Tay, going north-about into the Atlantic, when a twin-engined Heinkel 111 bomber swooped out of low cloud. The enemy plane came roaring in with her bomb doors open and machine-guns spraying lead. She dropped a single bomb, which exploded on the *Otterpool*'s port beam, harmlessly but close enough to send a shower of dirty water and shrapnel sweeping across the ship.

When the Heinkel came back for her second run, the *Otterpool*'s 12-pounder was manned and ready for action, but the gun was slow to traverse and its fire was ineffectual. The German bomber swooped again and again, knocking out the 12-pounder and wounding the two gunners with machine gun fire.

The *Otterpool* was now at the mercy of her attacker, prompt-ing Captain Prince to resort to defending his ship with the only gun he had to hand, his long-barrelled .303 Ross rifle. It was a ludicrous position, with Prince calling orders to the helmsman as he zig-zagged to avoid the Heinkel's bombs, at the same time defying it with his rifle. It was a situation that should have had only one end, as the Heinkel rained down as many as ten 250lb bombs. However, thanks to Captain Prince's skilful manoeuvring, none scored a direct hit.

The attack went on for more than half an hour, but was sud-denly ended with the appearance out of the clouds of three British fighters. The German pilot, realizing that the odds were against him, sheered away and ran for the horizon. Having suffered only superficial damage, and with her two wounded gunners being the only casualties, the *Otterpool* resumed her voyage.

Six months later, in June 1940, the *Otterpool* was homeward bound from the Mediterranean in Convoy HG 34 carrying Algerian iron ore for Middlesbrough. HG 34, comprising twenty-three loaded merchantmen escorted by two destroyers and a sloop, was sailing in seven columns abreast, with the *Otterpool* leading Column 5. Abreast of her in Column 4 was the Commodore's ship *Florian*, a British steamer on her maiden voyage. The convoy was listed as 'fast', and while the *Florian* and the majority of the other ships had no difficulty in maintaining the convoy speed, the *Otterpool* was struggling.

In the small hours of the morning of 19 June the convoy was 190 miles north-west of Cape Finisterre and crossing the Bay of Biscay. The ships were now within easy reach of the newly occupied U-boat bases in France, and danger threatened. However, HG 34 was also only thirty-six hours steaming from the protection of British naval patrols in the South-Western Approaches, and given an element of luck, the convoy was 'home and dry'. Unfortunately, that luck was about to run out.

It so happened that a few days earlier Dönitz had received intelligence that a large convoy carrying 25,000 Australian troops for Britain had sailed from Gibraltar and was heading north. The C-in-C U-boats had hurriedly gathered together a wolf pack and set up an ambush for the troopers. Included in the pack were U-30, with Fritz-Julius Lemp desperate to atone for sinking the *Athenia* on the first day of the war, and U-48, under the command of Hans Rudolf Rösing, who had temporarily replaced Herbert Schultze, then hospitalized with a stomach and kidney complaint.

During the course of laying the ambush for the northbound troop convoy, U-30, U-48 and U-51 sighted HG 34, which seemed to be an easy target. The U-boats promptly attacked the convoy, thereby raising the alarm. Word reached the troop convoy, which then made a radical change of course and steamed around the prepared ambush.

U-48 was first to make contact with HG 34, sighting the convoy just after midnight on the 19th. Wasting no time, Rösing attacked from seaward, sinking the 6,067-ton Norwegian motor vessel *Tudor*. Some two hours later, Rösing again broke through the escort screen and quickly despatched two British ships, the 3,164-ton *Baron Loudoun* and the *British Monarch* of 5,661 tons.

The element of surprise lost, it was not until the afternoon of the 20th, when HG 34 was some 270 miles due west of St Nazaire, that the next attack came. Frits-Julius Lemp in U-30 fired a spread of two torpedoes at the leading ships. One torpedo shaved the bows of the *Andalusian*, second ship of Column 4, while the other narrowly missed the stern of the *Otterpool*, at the head of Column 5. Neither ship was aware that she was under attack.

The *Otterpool* was the target of another near miss later in the day, when Dietrich Knorr in U-51 tried his luck. Again, Captain Tom Prince was completely unaware that his ship had been targeted, perhaps because he had more pressing needs on his mind. The *Otterpool's* well-worn engine, being pushed beyond its limits to maintain the increased convoy speed, was beginning to falter. Chief Engineer Tom West worked his magic for a while, but soon the beat of the pistons slowed, and Captain Prince was forced to pull out of line to allow the ships astern to overtake.

By nightfall the *Otterpool* was several miles behind the rear ships of HG 34 and dropping further back all the time. Captain Prince welcomed the approaching cloak of darkness, but it came too late. U-30 was stalking his ship, and at 1942 Lemp emptied his stern tube at her from close quarters.

The *Otterpool*, sagging under the weight of her cargo of 8,100 tons of iron ore, was doomed. Lemp's torpedo blasted open her hull, the sea poured into her half-empty holds and she sank like the proverbial stone. Captain Tom Prince and twenty-two of his crew went down with her, the sixteen men who survived being plucked from the sea several hours later by the sloop HMS *Scarborough*.

Captain Thomas Prince has no known grave other than the cold Atlantic. His passing was marked only by the following acknowledgement of his 'good services' which appeared in the *London Gazette* on 27 July 1940:

> I am commanded by the Lord Commissioners of the Admiralty to inform you that they have learnt with great satisfaction, through their recommendations the Prime Minister has obtained the King's approval for the publication of the name of the late Captain Thomas Prince in the London Gazette as commended for good services in the SS *Otterpool* when attacked by enemy aircraft.

Fritz-Julius Lemp's career flourished for another eighteen months, during which he sank a total of twenty Allied merchant ships, amounting to 96,639 tons gross, an achievement which earned him the Knight's Cross, Germany's highest award. His end came on 9 May 1941 when, in command of the long-range Type IXB U-110, he joined in a pack attack on the eastbound convoy OB 318 off Cape Farewell. OB 318 consisted of forty-three loaded merchantmen escorted by three destroyers, an Armed Merchant Cruiser, three corvettes and two anti-submarine trawlers of the 3rd Escort Group.

Despite the strength of the convoy's escort force, Lemp had already sunk two of its merchantmen and was seeking a third victim when U-110 was caught in the Asdic beam of the corvette HMS *Aubretia*. The destroyer HMS *Broadway* joined *Aubretia*, and the two escorts proceeded to smother the U-boat with depth charges. Seriously damaged, U-110 was forced to surface.

Fifteen of U-110's crew were killed by gunfire from the escorts, while Lemp and thirty-two others took to the water. It is believed that when Lemp was swimming away from the abandoned submarine he realized that the scuttling charges had failed to sink her. He was last seen swimming back towards U-110, presumably intending to re-board, and is assumed to have drowned in the attempt.

When it was realized that U-110 was not about to sink, the destroyer *Bulldog* sent a boarding party across, and the submarine was taken in tow. However, she sank before she could be brought into port, but before she went down her Enigma machine and code books had been found and taken off. They were sent to Bletchley Park, where they played a significant role in the breaking of the German naval codes.

CHAPTER THREE

Friday the Thirteenth

The war at sea was gathering pace when, on 28 September 1939, Convoy KJ 2 sailed from Kingston, Jamaica and set out to cross the Atlantic. Comprising twenty-five merchant ships, nineteen British, five French, and one Panamanian, of which ten were loaded tankers, KJ 2 was regarded as a convoy of the utmost importance, worthy of a strong escort. The ocean convoy system still being in its infancy, no surface escorts were available, and KJ 2 would have sailed unescorted had it not been that the giant French submarine *Surcouf* was in the West Indies and had been summoned home to France. She was assigned to be KJ 2's sole guardian for the crossing.

The *Surcouf* was the largest ocean-going submarine of her day, and regarded as equivalent to any conventional cruiser afloat. Displacing 3,250 tons on the surface, she was 361ft long, 29ft in the beam and proportionately armed. She mounted two 8-inch guns in a turret forward of her conning tower, two 1.5-inch AA guns aft and twelve torpedo tubes, with twenty-four torpedoes. A small reconnaissance float plane with foldable wings was carried in a hangar abaft the conning tower. Manned by a crew of 118, with a surface speed of 18½ knots and a maximum range of 10,000 miles, the *Surcouf* was a formidable warship, with the added advantage of being able to operate underwater. Sadly, like France's Maginot Line, she would eventually prove to be a 'white elephant', but for the moment she was fulfilling the role of an impressive deterrent to any potential enemy.

Eight days out from Kingston, KJ 2 unexpectedly ran into a dense fog bank. None of the ships in the convoy, not even their escort, was equipped with radar, and with twenty-six ships steaming blind in close proximity to each other, chaos ensued. Whistles screeched, engine room telegraphs clanged, near-collisions proliferated and the once orderly procession of ships became a rout.

The leading ship of the convoy's Column 7 was the French motor tanker *Emile Miguet*, under the command of Captain Robert

Andrade. Owned by Compagnie Française des Petroles of Paris, at 14,115 tons gross the *Emile Miguet* was a 'supertanker' of the 1930s, and like the escorting *Surcouf*, the largest of her class afloat. She was bound for Le Havre, and her cargo consisted of 137,000 barrels, or 18,690 tons, of crude oil and petroleum, a highly volatile mixture liable to explode if ill-used and turn the ship into a gigantic funeral pyre for her crew.

Acutely conscious of his ship's vulnerability, when the fog came down Captain Andrade decided to leave the convoy and press on alone. The *Emile Miguet* had a service speed of 13½ knots, and when Andrade rang for full speed, she surged forward, leaving the chaos of KJ 2 behind her. When the fog dispersed several hours later, the tanker had left the other ships far astern. Andrade debated whether or not to wait for the convoy to catch up, but the prospect of being able to once again go his own way and set his own course and speed proved to be too much of a temptation. The *Emile Miguet* carried on alone at full speed.

In the opening days of the war, Allied merchantmen sailing independently and unescorted in the North Atlantic had been easy targets for the waiting U-boats, who pounced on them with great enthusiasm. Fourteen ships totalling 83,344 tons gross were ruthlessly dispatched in just over one week. Now that the Admiralty had belatedly introduced escorted convoys, Dönitz decided the time was ripe to try out his *Rudeltaktik*, a dream born while he was a prisoner of war in the First World War. *Rudeltaktik* involved U-boats hunting in groups, which would later become known as 'wolf packs'.

Dönitz's fledgling wolf pack was made up of six boats, three Type VIIBs and three Type XIs, namely U-45 (Alexander Gelhaar), U-47 (Günter Prien), U-48 (Herbert Schultze), U-37 (Werner Hartmann), U-40 (Wolfgang Barten), and U-42 (Rolf Dau). Kapitän zur See Werner Hartmann in U-37 was to command the pack at sea. Five of the boats sailed from Kiel on 4 October 1939 and entered the North Atlantic via the north of Scotland, while the sixth, Wolfgang Barten's U-40, which had been delayed, was ordered to go southabout through the English Channel. At the time, Berlin was not aware that the British had mined parts of the Channel, and in the early hours of the 13th U-40 hit a mine off Dover and blew up with the loss of all but three of her crew. Dönitz's *Rudeltaktik* was off to a bad start.

Right from the outset of the war, the German Intelligence Service, B-Dienst, had been reading the British naval codes, and soon after the U-boat pack sailed, Dönitz received word that Convoy KJ 2 had left Kingston eastbound across the Atlantic. He immediately contacted U-37, ordering Hartmann to waylay the convoy as it neared the Western Approaches; but KJ 2 being delayed and dispersed by the mid-Atlantic fog bank, that planned attack never took place.

As for the *Emile Miguet*, the gods must have been smiling on her, as the fog that caused her to abandon her convoy lifted within hours, and thereafter she had forged eastwards at full speed in fine, clear weather, alone and unmolested by any enemy. As the sun went down on 12 October, she was only 360 miles due west of Land's End and less than forty-eight hours from her discharge port, Le Havre. Captain Andrade, pacing the bridge of the tanker with night approaching, had good reason to congratulate himself on having the foresight to go it alone. But he was shocked out of his pleasant reverie when the conning tower of a submarine suddenly reared up out of the water on the starboard bow. U-48, back at sea on her second war patrol, had found her first potential victim.

As soon as U-48's casings were dry, men spilled out of the forward hatch, and within minutes had manned, loaded and trained the 88mm deck gun. Without further hesitation, Herbert Schultze gave the order to open fire on the *Emile Miguet*, which was already attempting to flee to the north. U-boat's first shell exploded in the tanker's after accommodation, killing 18-year-old seaman Joseph Le Maou.

Other shells followed in quick succession, each one as well aimed as the first, slamming home in the *Emile Miguet*'s hull and upperworks. Fire broke out, and was spreading rapidly. Having no guns with which to hit back, and fearing his highly volatile cargo might explode at any minute, Captain Andrade bowed to the inevitable. In order to avoid any further casualties, he rang the engines to stop and ordered his men to abandon ship.

When it became clear that the tanker was being abandoned, Herbert Schultze ordered his gunners to cease fire. Thirty-seven of the *Emile Miguet*'s crew got away in two boats, leaving behind the bodies of Joseph Le Maou and one other man who was missing, believed killed. The survivors pulled well clear of the burning ship, then lay back on their oars to watch her sink. Neither they nor Herbert Schultze were aware that there was a witness to the attack.

Some six miles to the east, emerging out of the deepening twilight, came the *Heronspool*, making her way to the west after straggling so far astern of Convoy OB 17 that she was out of sight of the other ships. Realizing that he had no hope of rejoining the convoy, Captain Batson had also decided to carry on alone.

Batson was on the bridge with Chief Officer Charles Clifford when they sighted the pall of black smoke billowing skyward from the burning *Emile Miguet*. Both men raised their binoculars to investigate.

As they watched, a bright flash of gunfire was seen through the distant pall of smoke, and then the burning tanker came into view. Batson's first instinct was to go to the rescue of the stricken ship, but as he was about to alter course to bring her ahead, the tanker swung clear to reveal a submarine on the surface behind her.

Having served at sea in the First World War, the scene was all too familiar to Sydney Batson, and he knew he must look to the safety of his own ship and crew first. Ordering the helm hard to starboard, he gave a double ring on the engine room telegraph for emergency full speed.

The *Heronspool* was no ocean greyhound, but she responded to the urgency of the situation by turning short round and presenting her squat stern to the enemy. With black smoke belching from her tall funnel as her bare-chested firemen bent to their shovels, and a great frothing of wake, she took off to the north-east.

The *Heronspool*, a younger cousin of the *Firby*, built in the same West Hartlepool shipyard in 1929, was another typical north-east coast tramp, coal-fired, single screw, with five roomy cargo holds. Given a calm sea with a following wind, she was able to manage around 7½ to 8 knots, but no more. She would certainly break no records, thrill no hearts, but she was as solid and reliable as the men who manned her, a ship's company recently increased by one with the arrival on board of Able Seaman Gunner John Pearson RN (retired). Pearson, called out of retirement by the war, had arrived on board while the *Heronspool* was loading in Swansea, and with him had come a dockyard squad bearing two guns, a Mk IV 4-inch anti-submarine gun and a Mk V high-angle 12-pounder for use against aircraft. Both were relics of the Jutland era, having been kept in Admiralty storage for twenty years against the event of hostilities breaking out again. Overnight, the *Heronspool* had been transformed from a helpless merchantman into a ship with a sting in her tail.

In accordance with protocol, the guns were both mounted aft so that they could be used in defence only. Manned by trained naval gunners, no doubt they would have been a serious deterrent to any attacker, but in those early days of the war the Royal Navy had few gunners to spare. The solution envisaged was for Able Seaman Pearson to select suitable members of the *Heronspool's* crew to form gun's crews. This would be no easy matter. A merchant ship, being a commercial enterprise, carries the minimum of crew, each man having a specific job to do, and firing guns is not one of them.

When the *Heronspool* sailed from Swansea in the late afternoon of 6 October, she was on her summer marks with 8,000 tons of Welsh anthracite bound for Montreal. Unlike her usual cargo of steaming coal, which left her decks and upperworks covered in a thick layer of black dust, the hard anthracite was comparatively clean. After a quick sluice down with hoses, by the time the *Heronspool* arrived off Milford Haven at first light on the 7th, her paintwork shone again.

Milford Haven, being a fine, deep, natural harbour, was an ideal assembly point for convoys. The *Heronspool* lay to anchor there for the next three days, while other ships came in from Bristol Channel ports to form part of Convoy OB 17. She sailed again on 10 October in company with six other ships, including yet another from the Ropner stable, the 4,803-ton *Stonepool*, under the command of Captain Albert White. The *Stonepool*, also carrying coal, was bound south for the Cape Verde islands, where the Admiralty maintained a coaling station. Sydney Batson and Albert White were old shipmates, having sailed together in Ropner's ships for a number of years, but the only contact they could manage while at anchor in the haven was by signal lamp.

The seven ships comprising Convoy OB 17 hove in their anchors and left the shelter of Milford Haven just before sunrise on the 10th. It was a fine, clear autumn morning, but with a chill in the air presaging the approach of winter. Led by the vice commodore's ship *City of Sydney*, they filed past St Anne's Head and out into the open sea, where their destroyer escort was waiting.

The intention was for the seven ships to rendezvous off the Smalls Lighthouse in the St George's Channel, with other ships coming south from Liverpool. Escorted by the destroyers *Ilex* and *Imogen*, the enlarged convoy would then steam out into the Atlantic as far as longitude 26° W, some 750 miles due west of Land's End. There, beyond the effective range of the German U-boats – or so it was hoped – the ships would go their own separate ways, some west across the Atlantic, others south to the Cape and beyond. It was a good plan, but like so many good plans it went awry.

Unfortunately, the Liverpool contingent of OB 17 had been landed with a lame duck in the form of the Cardiff-registered tramp, 4,748-ton *Leeds City*, bound in ballast for Philadelphia. She appeared to be insufficiently ballasted, since her propeller was lifting partly out of the water as she dipped to the swells. Consequently, she was unable to maintain convoy speed, the other ships having to slow down from time to time to allow her to catch up. This led to the rendezvous off the Smalls being missed, the Milford Haven ships carrying on out to sea, while the Liverpool ships chased after them. The two sections finally came together at dusk on the 11th, but by the morning of the 12th the convoy was again in disarray. The convoy commodore, Vice Admiral A. E. Evans, sailing in the 4,824-ton *Bolton Hall*, reported:

> At daylight on the 12th (0645) *Leeds City* was 6 miles astern, *Heronspool*, *Stonepool*, *Glenlea*, *Ashbury* and *Diloma* not in sight. At 1300 on 12th *Diloma* was sighted 10 miles on port beam and was steaming a parallel course. There can be no excuse for her action. In earlier efforts to ascertain why this ship and the *Generton* had fallen astern had failed. Ships on station at point of dispersal at 1900 on 12th, *Bolton Hall*, *Seaforth*, *John Holt*, *Corrales*, *City of Sydney*, *Lobos*, *Generton*, and just astern, *Leeds City*.

Convoy OB 17, one of the earliest convoys of the Second World War, was not going according to plan. Vice Admiral Evans commented:

> The optimistic assessment of ships' speeds given by owners and/or Masters leads to serious delays in the arrival of faster ships at their destinations – furthermore, it makes station-keeping impossible and zig-zagging dangerous.

For the greater part of this voyage up to half the ships were left literally unescorted – the alternative in this case, to proceed at 7 knots or less, was not acceptable.

There could be much improvement in the conduct of a convoy if Masters ensured that after this, officers of watch had studied standing orders.

The practice of masters and owners declaring their ships to be capable of unrealistic speeds – for instance, the *Heronspool*'s owners had claimed she was a 10-knot ship – was common, and would haunt convoy commodores throughout the war. It was an understandable weakness, for both those who sailed and those who managed had pride in their ships, no matter how old and decrepit they might be, but it was a dangerous practice, nevertheless.

When the *Heronspool* had surprised U-48 in the act of attacking the *Emile Miguet,* and Captain Batson decided to run to the north-east, he was unsure whether or not his ship had been seen by the enemy, but he assumed the worst. He sent for Radio Officer George Haresnape and instructed him to transmit the submarine attack signal, SSS, followed by the ship's name and position. He then spoke to Chief Engineer Charles Dobson and explained the urgency of the situation. Beyond that, Batson could do no more than hope and pray that the approaching darkness would soon draw its cloak around his ship, hiding her from any pursuer.

To Batson's great relief, the night came quickly, but if he was looking for concealment he was disappointed. The moon was not yet up, but the sky was cloudless, and the myriad twinkling stars that sprawled from horizon to horizon were so bright that the *Heronspool* must have been clearly visible at a considerable distance.

The atmosphere on the bridge of the *Heronspool* was electric. Batson and Clifford had been joined by the Second and Third Officers, and the four men, along with a seaman on lookout in each wing of the bridge, were constantly sweeping the horizon, searching for any sign of the enemy. Radar was still only a fond dream for merchant ships, and the darkness was impenetrable to their tired eyes.

Below, in the engine room, where the thump-thump of the flashing pistons and the roar of the boiler furnaces drowned out all conversation, Chief Engineer Charles Dobson stood to with his juniors, eyes glued to the flickering dials. Dobson, having been torpedoed in the First World War, was conscious more than anyone of the terrible dangers they faced that night.

Aft, on the poop, Gunner John Pearson spoke quietly to his makeshift gun's crew gathered around the long-barrelled 4-inch, explaining what was required of them when the testing time came.

Every man jack of the *Heronspool*'s crew waited and hoped, and some prayed, while their ship took wings into the sanctuary of the night. Valiantly answering to the urgent beat of her engine, for the first time in her ten busy years afloat the *Heronspool* touched 10 knots as she zig-zagged frantically away from the unseen threat.

An hour went by, and with no sign of pursuit Captain Batson dared to speculate that perhaps the enemy submarine had been too busy shelling the French tanker to notice the approach of the *Heronspool*. But it was a vain hope, for U-48 was still out there, hidden by the darkness and following close in the British tramp's wake. When the U-boat's lookouts had first sighted the *Heronspool*, Herbert Schultze had submerged to periscope depth and watched her approach. When the tramp sheered away to the north-east, he left the *Emile Miguet* to her fate and gave chase, surfacing when darkness fell. U-48 was capable of 17½ knots on the surface and she quickly closed up on her quarry. Shortly before 2000, when the *Heronspool* was within range of his 88mm, Schultze, adhering strictly to the rules of warfare, put a warning shot across her bows.

The sudden crash of the gun and the column of water erupting on the *Heronspool*'s starboard beam put an end to Sydney Batson's dreams of escape. It also made him very angry, and he continued to run away from the enemy, zig-zagging wildly to spoil his aim.

The U-boat appeared to have dived again, and the night went quiet, the silence disturbed only by the loud beat of the *Heronspool*'s labouring engine and the swish of her bow-wave. Then, at about 2030, a signal lamp stabbed the darkness astern.

'What ship?' the lamp flashed. 'Stop!'

Captain Batson did not reply to the lamp, nor had he any intention of stopping his ship. Searching the horizon astern with his binoculars, he eventually detected a movement on the port quarter. At first it was just a vague shadow, but in the light of the stars it grew into the unmistakeable silhouette of a surfaced submarine. Without hesitation, Batson gave the order for the 4-inch to open fire.

Aft, on the poop gun platform, the long barrel of the gun was already traversing left on to the pursuing U-boat, which was now clearly visible just 400yds off the *Heronspool*'s port quarter. Gunner Pearson, who was laying the 4-inch, brought the target into his sights and squeezed the trigger. The gun thundered, spewing flame from its muzzle, recoiled sharply and was reloaded with remarkable speed by its crew of amateurs. A second shell followed hard on the heels of the first, both bursting within yards of U-48. Shaken by this unexpected show of resistance, Herbert Schultze recalled his gun's crew, cleared the conning tower and dived.

On the *Heronspool*'s bridge, Captain Batson watched with a grim smile on his lips as the U-boat disappeared, then hauled the ship around 90° to the west and continued to zig-zag away at full speed. The first round was his.

Another two hours went by with the *Heronspool* straining every rivet to escape under the cover of night. When, by 2300, there was still no sign of pursuit, and every man on board, from Captain Batson down to 14-year-old Galleyboy Frank Elders, had begun to believe they had shaken off their persistent attacker, U-48 suddenly surfaced again right astern. Without waiting for the order from the bridge, the 4-inch crew snapped off another two quick shots, only to see their target dip below the surface again.

Had the *Heronspool* been a naval vessel equipped with Asdic and depth charges she would have fought on equal terms with this elusive German, but each time U-48 dived the merchantman was struck blind. And so, for the next two hours the ill-matched adversaries fought a running battle, U-48 coming to the surface from time to time and lobbing 88mm shells at the fleeing ship. Gunner Pearson and his crew gave as good in return, firing whenever they sighted the submarine. They scored no hits, but they had the satisfaction of being able to retaliate in kind. John Pearson later said that if his gun's crew had received even the minimum of training, they were so keen that they would have matched the U-boat's fire and perhaps even have sunk her. As it was, they did their best, loading and firing like professionals. In fact, Pearson later commented that their rate of fire was so fast and sustained that parts of their gun platform had begun to fall off under the strain.

Midnight came, and the running fight went on into the new day. Ominously, it was Friday the Thirteenth; not a good day to be facing up to a vastly superior enemy. It was perhaps just as well that these gallant men who were flirting with death to save their ship were not aware of the danger they were in. German records show that U-48 had already fired five torpedoes at the *Heronspool*, the first at 2024 on the 12th, the second at 2115, the third at 2305, the fourth at 2350, and the fifth at 2352. All had missed their target, leaving Herbert Schultze so frustrated that he was debating whether or not to abandon the chase. He decided to try just once more, and at 0100 on the 13th his persistence was at last rewarded.

The sixth torpedo, fired from close range, hit the *Heronspool* forward of her bridge on the port side, blasting a great jagged hole in her hull plates through which the sea poured in to flood her forward holds. She immediately took on a heavy list to port and began to settle by the head.

Captain Sydney Batson, clinging white-knuckled to the bridge taffrail, was deafened by the explosion and showered with spray and burning debris. When he recovered from the initial shock, it was quickly obvious to him that his ship had not long to go. Reluctantly, he rang the engine room telegraph to *Finished with Engines* and then reached for the whistle lanyard to sound the *Abandon Ship*. Even this went wrong. At Batson's first tug on the lanyard the whistle jammed open, adding the terrifying screech of escaping steam to the general confusion. Right aft on the poop, the situation was even worse. As a result of the shock of the exploding torpedo the already disintegrating gun platform had collapsed altogether, and the 4-inch gun's crew were having great difficulty in extricating themselves from the wreckage.

Despite the general confusion, discipline held and the *Heronspool's* entire crew of thirty-six cleared the sinking ship in two lifeboats. Pulling away to a safe distance, they lay back on their oars and contemplated the disaster from which they had just escaped. It was a sad sight. Listing drunkenly to port, her shattered bow section clearly visible in the light of the stars, the *Heronspool* was plainly not long for this world.

Regretfully turning their backs on the stricken ship, the survivors hoisted sail and set course for the Irish coast, some 200 miles to the east. As they did so, the wind began to strengthen, and they knew that their next battle would be with the elements.

The new day dawned grey and threatening, but with the dawn came rescue in the form of the American passenger liner *President*

Harding. Under the command of Captain Roberts, and carrying 596 passengers, she had been on passage to New York when on the night of the 12th she intercepted the *Emile Miguet*'s SOS. Without a second thought, Roberts had steamed back 200 miles at full speed to the rescue, only to find the French tanker on fire and with her decks awash, but still afloat. There was no sign of her crew, which by then had been picked up by another American ship, the freighter *Black Hawk*.

The *President Harding* was already well behind her schedule, and there was no question of returning to a British port to land the *Heronspool*'s men, who would eventually be taken to New York. Meanwhile, their ordeal was not over. The worsening weather they had experienced while in their lifeboats became a roaring gale, and then a storm of such proportions that the 13,865-ton *President Harding* struggled to make any headway at all. Battered by mountainous seas, she lost a man overboard, and sixty-eight of her passengers were injured. Had Captain Batson and his men still been their boats when the storm struck, their fate might have been very different.

Shaken by his unexpected running battle with the *Heronspool*, Herbert Schultze exercised more caution when he approached his next victim just a few hours later. She was the 6,903-ton French steamer *Louisiane*.

Owned by Compagnie Générale Transatlantique of Paris, the *Louisiane* was treading a familiar path on her way from Antwerp to Havana, Cuba with a general cargo. She had left Southend in the Thames estuary six days earlier in Convoy OA 17 with twelve other ships, but had straggled astern a day or two out. When Schultze found her just after 0800 on the 13th, she was 350 miles west of Land's End and completely alone.

After examining the French ship through his periscope and satisfying himself that she was unarmed, Schultze had surfaced and stopped her with a warning shot. There had been no show of resistance, the *Louisiane*'s crew abandoning their ship without hesitation. As soon as their boats were clear, Schultze ordered his 88mm crew to open fire, and for the next ten minutes they pounded the *Louisiane* until she was a burning wreck. She capsized and sank at 0855. One member of her crew was lost, the remainder being picked up a few hours later by HMS *Imogen*, one of the escorting destroyers from the now dispersed Convoy OB 17.

The *Louisiane* had been easy meat for Herbert Schultze. Likewise Headlam's 3,677-ton *Sneaton*, another north-east coast tramp. The Whitby-registered ship was on passage from Cardiff to Rio de Janeiro with 4,300 tons of coal when Schultze sighted her in the Western Approaches around noon on the 14th. She was attempting the 5,000-mile voyage alone and unarmed. Schultze stopped her with a shot across her bows in the usual manner, and twenty minutes later, after her crew had taken to the boats, he sank her with a torpedo. Again, largely thanks to Schultze's humane approach, only one man was lost. The survivors were rescued by the Belgian tanker *Alexandria André* and landed at Weymouth.

Soon after sinking the *Sneaton*, Schultze received word of Hitler's decree of 4 October ordering all Allied shipping to be sunk on sight. There was to be no more surfacing, no more warning shots across the bow. Torpedoing from periscope depth with little or no risk to the attacking U-boat was to be the future. At last Herbert Schultze and his fellow U-boat commanders were free to use the great advantage the submarine gave them.

News of this abrupt change of tactics from the Queensberry Rules to total war had not yet reached Captain Francis Stenson aboard the 7,256-ton cargo liner *Clan Chisholm*, then in the Mediterranean on passage from Port Said to Gibraltar. When war was declared on 3 September, the *Clan Chisholm* had been loading her customary homeward cargo of produce in Indian ports; in this case, 1,750 tons of pig iron, 3,300 tons of tea, 1,900 tons of jute and 2,600 tons of general. In the Indian Ocean and Mediterranean the Clan liner sailed alone, and it was not until she reached Gibraltar on 11 October that the war became a reality for her.

In Gibraltar, the *Clan Chisholm* came under Admiralty orders and was instructed to join Convoy HG 3 for the passage north to Liverpool. When formed, HG 3 consisted of twenty-seven merchant ships, most of which were homeward bound with cargoes of produce from ports in the East. The majority were fast cargo liners like the *Clan Chisholm*, but there were a few old timers, even a couple of tramps, and as the speed of a convoy is dictated by its slowest ship, HG 3 was to go north at 9 knots. Furthermore, other than two destroyers to see them clear of the Mediterranean, the convoy would be unescorted until it reached the South-Western Approaches.

When Admiral Dönitz received word that a large British convoy of loaded ships was steaming north from Gibraltar without escort he immediately gathered together was left of his first wolf pack, now reduced to just three boats, Hartmann's U-37, Sohler's U-46 and Schultze's U-48. They met at a pre-arranged rendezvous point some 150 miles north-west of Cape Finisterre and lay in wait for HG 3.

Herbert Sohler in U-46 was first to sight the northbound convoy on the morning of the 17th. The ships were steaming in nine orderly columns abreast, still without an escort. The three waiting U-boats moved in that afternoon, Sohler opening the attack by torpedoing the 10,000-ton cargo/passenger liner *Yorkshire* carrying a full cargo from Rangoon and 151 passengers. Ellerman's *City of Mandalay* went to her aid, only to be hit by another of Sohler's torpedoes. She sank with the loss of seven lives. The *Yorkshire*, meanwhile, was still afloat, but not for much longer. Werner Hartmann in U-37 put her out of her misery, sending her to the bottom with the loss of twenty-five crew and thirty-three passengers.

Night had fallen by the time Herbert Schultze was in position to attack HG 3. He set his sights on one of the outriders, the two-year-old cargo liner *Clan Chisholm*, and at 2032 fired a single torpedo. Unfortunately for Schultze, the torpedo failed to detonate and bounced off the *Clan Chisholm*'s hull, sinking harmlessly to the bottom. Those on her bridge heard a dull thump when the torpedo hit, but took no notice. Three minutes later, however, when Schultze's second torpedo exploded in her engine room, they knew that their long voyage home from India had come to a premature end. Four of the *Clan Chisholm*'s engine room crew were killed, and her bottom cargo of pig iron caused her to sink in just a few minutes. Captain Stenson and forty-one of his crew were picked up by the Swedish motor vessel *Bardaland*, seventeen others were rescued by the small Norwegian whaler *Skudd I*, and the remaining fifteen, after four days adrift in their lifeboat, were found and rescued by the Union Castle liner *Warwick Castle*.

The coordinated attack on HG 3 by the remnants of Dönitz's first wolf pack was not a major disaster for Allied shipping, but it was bad enough, resulting in the loss of three first-rate ships and their cargoes, along with sixty-nine lives. It might have been much worse, were it not for the fact that all three U-boats involved were running short of fuel and torpedoes, resulting in their being ordered home by Dönitz.

With regard to HG 3, the question might be asked why these important ships were sailing without escort in waters accessible to the U-boats. More to the point, why were they sailing in convoy at all? The majority of the ships were fast cargo liners, the *Clan Chisholm*, for example, was a twin-screw ship capable of 17 knots. Yet they were crawling north at 9 knots, a speed dictated by HG 3's slowest member, the Bristol Channel tramp *Uskmouth*. Logically, the *Clan Chisholm* and the others capable of outrunning the U-boats should have been sailing independently, and at full speed. It is true to say that during the course of the war the Lords of the Admiralty often moved in mysterious ways.

CHAPTER FOUR

Retribution

When, in the small hours of the morning of 13 October, the *Heronspool* finally ran out of sea room and succumbed to Herbert Schultze's torpedo, her sister ship and ex-convoy companion *Stonepool* was only 100 miles or so to the south-east. The 4,803-ton *Stonepool*, under the command of Captain Albert White and carrying 6,600 tons of Welsh steaming coal from Barry for St Vincent in the Cape Verde Islands, had also failed to keep up with Convoy OB 17. When there no longer seemed any point in attempting to rejoin the other ships, Captain White, like Captain Batson, had decided to carry on alone.

The *Stonepool's* wireless operator had picked up the *Heronspool's* initial SSS transmission of the night of the 12th, and thereafter had kept Captain White informed of the other ship's struggle to evade the attacking U-boat. White and Batson were old friends, having served together in several of Ropner's ships on their way up to command, and there was a strong bond between them.

Powerless to offer help, Albert White remained a silent witness to the pursuit and eventual destruction of the *Heronspool*, an event that left him both sad and angry. The *Stonepool* had also been defensively armed while in Barry, being fitted with similar leftovers from the Great War, a 4-inch and a 12-pounder, both mounted aft. These guns were in the care of Acting Leading Seaman George Hayter, another Royal Navy pensioner recalled to the colours. Hayter's ad hoc gun's crew consisted of Third Officer Leonard Corney, who had attended a three-day gunnery course before sailing and 62-year-old Chief Steward John Shipman, who had served as a merchant seaman gunner in the First World War, plus anyone else who was not on watch or otherwise engaged when the call came for Action Stations. It was a loose arrangement and yet to be tested. Had there been time for a few practice shoots, Captain White might have considered going to the *Heronspool's* aid; in any case, there was no way in which the *Stonepool's* worn out old engine could have got her there in time to intervene.

Captain White was not alone in listening in to the *Heronspool*'s calls for help. Also in the vicinity was U-42, whose commander, 33-year-old Kapitänleutnant Rolf Dau, was following the chase closely.

U-42 was one of the eight original Type IX long range boats built with distant waters in mind. Displacing 1,032 tons surfaced, 251ft long and 21ft in the beam, she was powered by two M.A.N. supercharged, 4-stroke, 9-cylinder diesels and two Siemens-Schukert double-acting electric motors, giving her 18.2 knots on the surface and 7.7 knots submerged. Capable of operating at depths of up to 750ft, she had a maximum range of 10,000 miles at 10 knots. Her armament was equally formidable: six torpedo tubes, four in the bow and two at the stern, a 105mm gun forward of the conning tower and a 37mm AA gun and twin 20mm cannon aft. On deck she carried ten torpedoes in five external containers, which were additional to the twenty-two torpedoes she carried below decks. In all, the Type IXs were a very powerful and versatile addition to Dönitz's U-boat fleet, but as the war progressed they proved to be vulnerable in that their size made them difficult to manoeuvre and slow to dive in an emergency. U-42 was about to be tested.

U-42 was the first of Admiral Dönitz's prototype wolf pack to arrive in the Western Approaches. Built by AG Weser in Bremen, and commissioned by Rolf Dau on 15 July 1939, she had spent over two months working up in the Baltic before sailing from Wilhelmshaven on her first war patrol on 2 October. Entering the Atlantic via the north of Scotland, her arrival in the Western Approaches had coincided with Commodore Evans' decision to disperse Convoy OB 17 at 1900 on the 12th.

U-42 was marking time on the surface some 330 miles west-south-west of Land's End when, just as the sun was lifting from the horizon on the 13th, the *Stonepool* came in sight. Called to the conning tower, Rolf Dau examined the approaching ship through his powerful binoculars. She was very deep in the water with very little bow-wave showing, indicating she was making no more than 7 or 8 knots. Furthermore, there was no sign of any escort. U-42's first sighting of the enemy appeared to show a fat plum ripe for the plucking. Dau decided not to waste a torpedo, and sent his men on deck to man the 105mm.

On the bridge of the *Stonepool*, Chief Officer Peter Love was crouched over the standard compass about to take a bearing of the rising sun to establish the compass error, when he became aware of a small object silhouetted against the hardening horizon. At first he thought it was the funnel of a ship hull-down, or perhaps a fishing trawler out from Ireland, but as the light grew and he focused his binoculars, he realized that he was looking at a submarine on the surface. Love sent the standby helmsman below to call Captain White.

White was on the lower bridge, washed and shaved and contemplating the arrival of the new day. The sky was clear blue with just a sprinkling of fluffy fine-weather clouds tinged red by the rising sun, the wind was a light breeze from the west and the sea was a millpond, disturbed only by a low south-westerly swell. It was a day full of promise.

The Captain's morning reverie was rudely interrupted when the standby man came clattering down the ladder from the bridge calling excitedly. At the word 'Submarine!' White brushed past the seaman and took the ladder two steps at a time. As he arrived on the bridge, U-42, now just 3 miles off on the port beam, put an accurately aimed shot across the *Stonepool*'s bows, the shell landing a mere 30yds ahead of the ship and sending up a tall spout of water.

With the acrid fumes from the explosion in his nostrils, Captain White knew he was faced with a very limited choice. This was the enemy, and he could either stop and haul down his flag, or run and make a fight of it. He also realized that if he chose to fight, the odds were stacked very heavily against the *Stonepool*. She was an ageing tramp to which anything over 8 knots did not come easily, and she was armed with an equally aged 4-inch manned by a largely untrained crew, whose only acquaintance with the gun so far was in polishing its brasswork. On the other hand, White mused, Leading Seaman Hayter and Chief Steward John Shipman were professionals, if somewhat out of practice. Then there was his 'Gunnery Officer', Third Officer Corney, who had at least been exposed to the rudiments of gunnery while attending his brief course held in a derelict warehouse in Barry Docks. Albert White, being a typically stubborn Yorkshireman, and an angry one at that, opted to run and fight.

Ordering the helmsman to put the wheel hard over to starboard, White reached for the whistle lanyard and sounded the signal for Action Stations. The core members of the *Stonepool's* make-shift gun's crew, Leading Seaman Hayter, Third Officer Corney and Chief Steward Shipman, were already on deck, and before the urgent screech of the steam whistle had died away, they were racing aft to their gun. Within two minutes of Captain White's sounding the alarm, the three men were on the gun platform and ready to open fire.

Sluggish to answer the helm due to the great weight of coal she was carrying, the *Stonepool* seemed to take an age to swing sufficiently to bring the U-boat on to the port quarter, where it was visible to those manning the 4-inch. Only then did the long-barrelled gun thunder and recoil as the *Stonepool's* first shell fired in anger went singing through the air towards the enemy. It fell short, but close enough to send up a curtain of spray that momentarily hid U-42 from sight.

With the fall of her first shell, the *Stonepool's* radio transmitter burst into life as her wireless operator sent out the prearranged call for help: SSS three times, followed by the ship's name and position. It took only seconds to send, but U-42's operator was listening and reported the message to Kapitänleutnant Dau, who at once ordered his gunners to bring down the *Stonepool's* wireless aerial. The thick copper wire stretched between the British ship's tall masts remained defiantly untouched, but one of U-42's salvo of 105mm shells went home in her forward hold, exploding with a dull thump.

There was no indication that any serious damage had been done, but to Captain White, who was facing aft and calling out helm orders as he swung the ship to dodge the fall of the ene-my's shot, it soon became apparent that all was not well. Each time the *Stonepool's* helm went over, she seemed slower to respond, and White's years of experience in conning ships told him that she was trimming by the head. He sent Chief Officer Love forward to assess the damage, and the news Love brought back was not good. U-42's shell had blown a jagged hole in the ship's side, only inches above the waterline, and each time she dipped to the swell the sea poured into her breached hold.

To repair the damage would involve shifting many tons of coal, and even then it might not be possible to patch the plating from inside. Meanwhile, the chase continued, with the *Stonepool* weaving and dodging, running like a frightened rabbit to evade the blast of the farmer's shotgun. But in this case, the rabbit was hitting back. Firing over open sights and without the luxury of a range finder, aiming the 4-inch was largely a matter of guesswork for John Hayter, but backed up by Corney and Shipman, he was answering shot with shot, and his shells were falling closer and closer to the pursuing U-boat.

The running fight went on for more than five hours, during which time Chief Engineer Richard Parsons was at the controls in the engine room making maximum use of every pound of steam his sweating firemen coaxed out of the *Stonepool*'s boilers. There is no record of what speeds the plucky little tramp achieved as she ran from her Armageddon, but no matter how hard U-42 tried, she failed to overtake her.

Had the two contestants been evenly matched, the fight might have ended differently, but the *Stonepool* presented a large and slow moving target hard to miss, while U-42, with just her conning tower and casings above the water, was fast and highly manoeuvrable. Furthermore, her gunners were trained naval men manning a modern weapon, one of AG Krupp's finest, and of larger calibre than the *Stonepool*'s 4-inch. The result of the fight should have been a foregone conclusion, and it almost was.

By now, U-42's gunners had got the range and, despite Captain White's erratic zig-zagging, their shells were falling uncomfortably close. One burst close on her port side abreast the engine room, and when the smoke and spray cleared, it could be seen that all that remained of the *Stonepool*'s port lifeboat was a pile of smouldering matchwood, thus reducing by fifty per cent the chances of survival for her crew.

As White continued to weave and dodge he saw the U-boat, now only a few hundred yards astern, suddenly submerge, and he braced himself for what he feared would happen next. The minutes ticked by, then a line of bubbles racing towards the ship confirmed his worst fears. Torpedo!

In fact, Rolf Dau, frustrated by the continued resistance of his intended victim, had fired a spread of four torpedoes from his bow tubes. Four 1½ ton missiles, each packed with 1,000lbs of high explosive and racing through the water at 30 knots, were homing in on the *Stonepool*'s starboard quarter. If just one of these torpedoes found their target it could mean the end for the British ship, but the sun was shining on her that morning. Captain White glimpsed the feathered track of one of them heading straight for his ship, and with seconds to spare wrenched the *Stonepool* out of the way. The torpedo porpoised briefly as it shot across the bow, and then disappeared. What happened to the other three is a matter of conjecture. They either sank before they reached their target, or veered off course to sink harmlessly at the end of their run.

Unwillingly to waste any more of his expensive torpedoes, Rolf Dau brought U-42 back to the surface and sent his gunners on deck again with orders to put an end to what was becoming, to his mind, a ridiculous farce.

In the hope of landing a crippling blow on the defiant British tramp, the German gunners increased their rate of fire, and a veritable rain of shells fell on and around the *Stonepool*. Fires were started on deck, one man was wounded by shrapnel and the starboard and only remaining lifeboat went the way of the port boat, blown clean out of its davits.

These were serious blows to the running ship, and confident that he now had the upper hand, Dau made the mistake of crossing the *Stonepool*'s stern, thus putting U-42 broadside on to the tramp's gunners. This was the opportunity Leading Seaman Hayter had been waiting for, and he was quick to take advantage. Firing as fast as they could load, the 4-inch crew hurled shell after shell at the U-boat. In the heat of the moment nobody could say whether any hits were scored, but there were certainly some very near misses, the spray thrown up by the exploding shells sometimes hiding the enemy from view.

Whatever transpired, Dau panicked and dived without warning his men on deck. The U-boat went down in a flurry of foam, leaving his gun's crew struggling in the water. Ten minutes later, realizing his mistake, Dau resurfaced and was seen to be rescuing his gunners. It was also evident to those on the bridge of the *Stonepool* that the U-boat's deck gun had been hit by one of the tramp's shells. The gun was lying on its side with its barrel trailing in the water. Dau had apparently had enough, and as soon as his gunners were back on board, he dived.

Uncertain whether or not the U-boat had gone away, Captain White continued on his north-easterly course at full speed for another half an hour. Then, assuming the threat had passed, he resumed course for the Cape Verde islands, where he had a cargo to deliver. However, it soon became apparent that the *Stonepool* was seriously down by the head. The Cape Verdes were still 2,000 miles away, and with both lifeboats destroyed by the shelling he had no means of abandoning ship if she sank. Reluctantly, he reversed course again to return to the nearest British port.

With water still flooding into her No.1 hold, the *Stonepool* became more sluggish to answer the helm as she steamed on a north-easterly course at 9 knots, and it became apparent to Captain White that unless something was done to stem the leak, his ship might well sink before she reached British waters. Chief Officer Love went forward with a party, the hatch was opened up and a start made on clearing away the coal to access the leak. A second party supervised by Chief Engineer Parsons began constructing a wooden patch on deck. At about 1500, while the work was still proceeding, smoke was seen on the horizon ahead heralding the arrival of the destroyers *Ilex* and *Imogen*. They had been heading for home following the dispersal of Convoy OB 17 when they received the *Stonepool*'s SSS message, and they had responded at full speed.

The arrival of the 35-knot I-class destroyers, each armed with four 4.7-inch guns and multiple racks of depth charges, must have been a huge boost to the flagging morale of the *Stonepool*'s crew. Weary after their long-drawn out running gunfight with the U-boat, they been alone on an empty ocean, without means of escape from their slowly sinking ship, and without hope. Now, with *Imogen* scouting ahead and *Ilex* bringing up the rear, their Asdics pinging as they swept underwater and their guns manned, survival seemed assured. Unknown to anyone in the little convoy, however, they were still being shadowed.

At about 1700, with the sun low on the horizon, there was a shout from the *Stonepool*'s masthead lookout. His outstretched arm pointed to two points abaft the port beam, where he had spotted a submarine surfacing. Captain White immediately passed the report to *Imogen* by Aldis lamp, and the escorting destroyers raced in to attack.

It is not clear why U-42 chose to surface then, but it seems likely that, due to damage inflicted by the *Stonepool*'s gunners, Kapitänleutnant Dau had no other option. In any event, seeing *Ilex* and *Imogen* approaching at full speed intent on his destruction, Dau quickly revised his decision and dived again.

Arriving over the spot where U-42 was seen to dive, *Ilex* and *Imogen* saturated the area with depth charges, forcing Dau to go deep in an attempt to escape. He took the boat down to 390ft before levelling off and creeping away, but his efforts were in vain. The British destroyers had locked on to U-42 with their Asdics, and they continued the attack. One of their charges exploded close to U-42's stern, blasting open her after ballast tanks. This caused the U-boat to 'stand on her head', with her bows reaching up at a 45° angle. To counteract this, Dau blew all his remaining ballast tanks, which resulted in U-42 breaking the surface like an emerging whale.

Ilex and *Imogen* opened fire with every gun they could bring to bear, scoring a number of hits forward of the U-boat's conning tower. Holed fore and aft, stopped and rolling in the swell, with the sea lapping over her casings, U-42 was at the mercy of the destroyers' guns. *Ilex*, seeing the opportunity for a kill, increased to full speed and went in to ram. This proved unnecessary, for the U-boat was obviously sinking, and at the last minute *Ilex* went full astern and merely grazed U-42's hull. This was the signal for the U-boat's crew to abandon ship by diving over the side. *Imogen* picked up seventeen men, including Kapitänleutnant Rolf Dau. The remaining thirty-two members of the crew went down with their boat.

With her leak temporarily stemmed, and with at least one of the destroyers escorting at all times, the *Stonepool* reached the safety of the Bristol Channel some thirty-six hours later and was taken into dry dock in Barry for repair. The *Stonepool*'s gun duel with U-42 went on record as the first action of the Second World War between a defensively equipped merchant ship and a U-boat which led directly to the sinking of the enemy. For his 'resolute and skilful action' in saving his ship, Captain Albert White was awarded the OBE, while Acting Leading Seaman George Hayter received the BEM with recommendation for early promotion to Leading Seaman.

Commenting on this 'resolute and skilful action', an entry appeared in the War Diary of the BdU (*Befehlshaber der U-boote* – Commander-in-Chief Submarines):

The risks which the boat runs in a gun action with an armed merchant vessel. One hit may render the boat incapable of diving and therefore the certain prey of destroyers. (It is not surprising that circumstances are different from those in the world war. At that time steamers were only gradually being armed; today all this has apparently been carefully planned and the effect of this form of defence must therefore be expected to be greater).

Of its nature the U-boat is intended to fight with torpedoes and not with guns. Her strength is in being able to make a surprise attack and her protection in deep diving. A full-scale torpedo attack always promises success; a gun action, which is always full-scale as soon as the boat is within range of the enemy guns, does not by any means promise the same results. Nevertheless, it must not be forgotten that she needs her guns to stop the ship and break resistance when she is not from the first in position to fire a torpedo at the enemy. It takes a long time to haul ahead and it is not always possible. To renounce the use of guns altogether would therefore lower the chances of success considerably.

Less than a month after the meeting with U-42, the *Stonepool* was back at sea again with her broached hull plates renewed, shuttling cargoes back and forth across the Atlantic. Ten months later, with a new crew and under the command of Captain Joseph Nicholson, she was in convoy, beating back across the North Atlantic down to her marks with a full cargo of grain topped off by Army trucks on deck. In the meantime, her defensive armament had been substantially increased by the addition of a 12-pounder and six heavy machine guns, along with fifteen fully trained DEMS gunners, a far cry from the small band of enthusiastic amateurs who under Acting Leading Seaman George Hayter had defied U-42. Given the opportunity, the *Stonepool* should now be able to more than hold her own against any enemy that challenged her.

Despite lessons learned at considerable cost in the First World War, in 1939 the Admiralty was again reluctant to introduce escorted convoys for Allied merchantmen in the North Atlantic. Eventually, a compromise was found which involved ships sailing under escort in the Western Approaches, where the threat from U-boats was greatest, followed by an ocean passage unescorted or under the doubtful protection of a single armed merchant cruiser when one was available.

In the early stages of the war this seemed to suffice, but after the fall of France in June 1940, the situation changed dramatically. Convoys were now under threat for the whole of the Atlantic crossing, and they required substantial escorts. Due to heavy losses suffered at Dunkirk and in Norway, the Royal Navy was unable to provide adequate protection, and this led to the formation of the Newfoundland Escort Force, which consisted of six Royal Canadian Navy destroyers and seventeen corvettes, backed up by seven destroyers, three sloops and five corvettes of the Royal Navy. Commanded by Commodore Leonard Murray RCN, the force was under the overall control of the C-in-C Western Approaches and provided escorts for convoys from Newfoundland to a point south of Iceland, where the Royal Navy took over.

The United States of America was still officially neutral, but as most of the cargoes carried by the convoys were of American origin, President Roosevelt decided it was in America's best interests to lend a hand; and while American troops took over the occupation of Iceland from British forces, in the spring of 1941 ships of the US Navy had begun unofficially escorting Allied convoys as far as Icelandic waters.

Convoy SC 42, made up of sixty-five merchant ships escorted by a destroyer and three corvettes of the 24th Canadian Escort Group, had sailed from Sydney, Cape Breton on 30 August 1941, bound east across the North Atlantic. The majority of the merchantmen were ageing tramps of uncertain capability, and it was not surprising that when, a few days out of Sydney, they ran into heavy weather, the 7½-knot designated speed of the convoy proved to be over-optimistic. Most of the time, the convoy was in disarray and struggling to maintain even 5 knots. In an ocean now teeming with Dönitz's U-boats, this was tempting Providence. The *Stonepool*, stationed at the head of Column 1, the outer column on the port side, was particularly vulnerable, and Captain Nicholson had posted extra lookouts and kept his guns fully manned day and night.

The expected attack came on the night of the 9th, when the convoy was south of Greenland's Cape Farewell. Waiting in ambush were fifteen U-boats of the wolf pack codenamed

Markgraf, and when the moon rose, SC 42 received a severe mauling, losing seven ships and their cargoes. In the hope of avoiding complete annihilation of the convoy, later in the morning of the 10th its escort was reinforced by the arrival of two more Canadian corvettes. At about the same time, *Markgraf* was joined by U-207, bringing the pack up to sixteen.

U-207, a new Type VIIC commissioned in Kiel only three months earlier by 25-year-old Oberleutnant zur See Fritz Meyer, was on her first war patrol, having sailed from Trondheim on 24 August. Meyer was also untried in combat, his only previous experience in command being eight months with U-34 while she was a training boat in the Baltic. Young to be in command of a U-boat, Meyer had yet to prove himself.

In the early hours of the 11th U-207 had penetrated SC 42's escort screen and was in position on the port side of the convoy near the leading ships. The *Stonepool,* at the head of the outer column, was first to cross Fritz Meyer's sights. He targeted her with a spread of four torpedoes from his bow tubes.

The bridge of the *Stonepool* was a place of shadows, the only light the shaded glow of the compass binnacle, the silence disturbed only by the crash of the waves and the click of the wheel as the helmsman fought to meet them. Captain Nicholson and the officer of the watch, Second Officer John Knight, conversed in hushed tones, their eyes never leaving the dark horizon outside. In the wings of the bridge the duffel-coated gunners fingered their weapons, watching the same horizon for any sign of danger. This was a ship on full alert, yet in the darkness of the night no one saw the thin trail of bubbles heralding the arrival of one of Fritz Meyer's torpedoes.

The torpedo struck just after midnight, smashing its way into the *Stonepool*'s engine room on her starboard side. To those on the bridge, the explosion was a dull thump that might have been just another wave slamming against the ship's side, but to those on watch below it was like a roar of thunder followed by an angry torrent of water as the sea cascaded into the *Stonepool*'s most vulnerable space. Within minutes the bottom plates were awash, the water level rising at an alarming rate and sealing the fate of all those trapped below.

Drifting engineless and in complete darkness, the *Stonepool* slewed beam-on to wind and sea. Each time she rolled she leaned further and further over to starboard, until she was almost on her beam ends. The abandon ship order given by Captain Nicholson was irrelevant; those still alive were already running for the boat deck. When they finally reached the deck they found that the starboard lifeboat was missing, blown away by the blast of the torpedo, and due to the severity of the list, it was impossible to launch the other boat on the port side. Five men, led by Able Seaman H. Matthews, clawed their way forward and released the port liferaft, following it over the side. They drifted clear just as the *Stonepool* finally gave up the fight, rolled over, and sank. Only three minutes had elapsed since she was torpedoed. In all, only seven survivors were picked up some two hours later by the corvette HMCS *Moosejaw*. Captain Joseph Nicholson, thirty-three of his crew and eight DEMS gunners lost their lives.

Shortly after the *Stonepool* was hit, another of Fritz Meyer's torpedoes sank Moss Hutchinson's 4,924-ton *Berury*, bringing up the rear of Column 11. As dawn was breaking, Meyer torpedoed and damaged the small Canadian steamer *Randa*. For the inexperienced Meyer, with a new and as yet untried boat, this was an auspicious start, but only the prelude to his end. Later in the day, a Catalina flying boat patrolling over the convoy surprised U-207 on the surface. The destroyers HMS *Leamington* and *Veteran*, another addition to SC 42's escort, answered the aircraft's alarm call and arrived to find U-207 still on the surface. When they came racing in at 22 knots to attack, Meyer crash-dived, but he could not evade the probing Asdics of the destroyers. *Leamington* and *Veteran* dropped a total of twenty-one depth charges over the spot where the U-boat had disappeared, and U-207 was never heard of again. Her active participation in the Battle of the Atlantic had lasted exactly eighteen days.

CHAPTER FIVE

Ropner's Again

After sinking the *Clan Chisholm* off Cape Finisterre on 17 October, Herbert Schultze decided it was time for U-48 to head home. She had by then been at sea for three weeks and had sunk five British merchant ships amounting to nearly 40,000 tons gross, a fair result for her first patrol of the war. In addition, the boat had almost exhausted her stock of torpedoes and was running low on fuel and provisions. Schultze radioed Wilhelmshaven to that effect, and duly received permission to return. Course was set to pass outside Ireland, around Scotland and into the North Sea, a 1,500-mile trek through waters teeming with British warships. No picnic. But first there was one more appointment to keep, and an unwelcome one at that. U-48 was 350 miles due west of Land's End and heading north when, on 19 October, yet another of those troublesome Ropner tramps crossed her path.

The 4,889-ton *Rockpool*, under the command of 46-year-old Captain William Harland, was on passage from Halifax, Nova Scotia to Newport, Mon. with 8,520 tons of iron ore. She was pure deadweight, with her summer marks awash and her owners rubbing their hands at the thought of the fat freight she would earn. Those who sailed in the *Rockpool* were not so enthusiastic. Their poor overburdened ship steered like a crab, and from the outset was hard-pressed to maintain convoy speed. One small consolation was that Convoy HX 4, which comprised only ten merchantmen, was well escorted by the heavy cruiser HMS *York*, the Canadian destroyer *Fraser* and the auxiliary minelayer HMS *Teviot Bank*.

The North Atlantic was running true to form. Soon after they cleared the coast of Newfoundland, the weather deteriorated steadily, until by dawn on the 13th it was blowing a full gale from the south-east, with a high, confused head sea made worse by the long Atlantic swells rolling in from the west. With their decks continuously awash with foaming water, the heavily laden merchantmen laboured hard to maintain steerage way, but they were fighting a losing battle, and the convoy was beginning to drift apart.

The *Rockpool*, stiff with the weight of the ore low down in her holds, was taking it badly, rolling and pitching like a demented soul, her scuppers streaming as they shed the water she was taking on deck. At times she resembled a half-tide rock. And in the midst of all this the engine room reported that they had a blown boiler tube and would have to stop to make repairs.

The night that followed was one not to be forgotten. Wisely, Captain Harland refused his chief engineer's request to stop and insisted in keeping the engine ticking over so that he could at least hold the *Rockpool* into the wind, thus minimizing the damage done by the seas breaking aboard.

When daylight finally and reluctantly came, the *Rockpool* was under way once more, but she was alone on an empty sea, the rest of the convoy being somewhere ahead out of sight. An inspection of the decks revealed no serious damage other than that one of her two lifeboats, having been hit by a wave, was hanging suspended by one fall. The boat was secured to prevent further damage.

The prospect of crossing the Atlantic alone did not deter Captain Harland. Before sailing on the outward passage, the *Rockpool* had been fitted with two guns, a 4-inch and a 12-pounder, both mounted aft. With the guns had come Colour Sergeant Thomas Watkins, Royal Marines (retired), who had formed a gun's crew from the ship's company consisting of Chief Steward George Wilson and Cook J. Hall, both of whom had attended a two-day gunnery course before sailing, 17-year-old Apprentice Hudson and anyone else who was off watch and interested. During the outward voyage Captain Harland had insisted on regular practice shoots, and Sergeant Watkins' gun's crew had achieved considerable accuracy. It might be said that Harland was almost spoiling for a fight. But then the Captain was no stranger to war.

William Herbert Harland, born in the North Riding of Yorkshire in 1893, first went to sea in 1908, serving as an officer apprentice with a Cardiff-based shipping company. When he completed his apprenticeship in 1914 he served briefly as a junior officer; but even though war had broken out, officers' berths at sea were still at a premium, and he soon found himself without a ship. Ashore and unemployed, Harland became caught up in the prevailing patriotic fervour and volunteered for Kitchener's Army.

In April 1915 Private William Harland landed in France with the 8th Battalion of the Durham Light Infantry, just in time to be rushed to the front for the Second Battle of Ypres. Thrown into the fight, the raw battalion suffered heavy casualties, Harland being among the wounded. Undeterred, after having his wound dressed, he returned to the front, but was again wounded, this time seriously.

William Harland's wounds were slow to heal, and in August 1917 he was discharged from the Army as 'being no longer physically fit for war service'. Unwilling to stay at home, and having already served his apprenticeship at sea, Harland sat for his Second Mate's Certificate at the Board of Trade, which he passed in December 1917. By this time the war had taken a heavy toll of officers in the merchant navy, and he had no difficulty in finding a ship. In January 1918 he signed on the 3,083-ton Whitby collier *John H. Barry* as Second Officer.

After a spell carrying coal to Russia for the Admiralty, in March 1918 the *John H. Barry* was sent into the Mediterranean to pick up a cargo of iron ore consigned to Barrow from the Tunisian port of La Goulette. She then joined a Gibraltar-bound convoy consisting of ten ships all similarly loaded. The convoy was somewhat bizarrely escorted by the converted yacht USS *Yankton*, the US Coastguard cutter *Ossipee*, HMS *Privet* and HMS *Acton*, two ex-merchant 'Q' ships, the French armed trawler *Chassiron* and the naval tug *Alice*. Lieutenant Commander J. C. Connor in the *Yankton* was Senior Officer Escort.

Steaming in four columns of two ships and two columns of one, the convoy set off at 7½ knots, but as darkness fell the weather deteriorated sharply. The night was moonless, with a heavy overcast and blinding rain squalls, and the ships soon became scattered. At dawn on 17 March the *John H. Barry* was 12 miles astern of the other ships and was being escorted by HMS *Acton* and the tug *Alice*. Two miles further west again were two other British ships, the *Garyvale* and the *Ivydene*. At about 0500 the *Garyvale* reported that two torpedoes had been fired at her, both of which missed. The convoy's escorts searched the area, but found no evidence of an enemy submarine.

The convoy, having re-formed, continued to the west, completely unaware that Oberleutnant Otto Launburg at the periscope of UB 52 was watching and waiting for the opportunity to strike again.

This did not come until 0630, when it was fully light. The *Ivydene*, back in position at the head of the second column, was hit amidships on her port side by a torpedo. She remained afloat for some time, during which all her crew except one man were rescued unharmed.

Having thus made his presence known, Otto Launburg then withdrew, returning again that night. At 0120 on the 18th the *John H. Barry*, which had also rejoined the convoy and was leading Column 3, was hit by a torpedo on her starboard side. She immediately veered to starboard, collided with one of the ships in the adjacent column and sank within five minutes. Three men went down with her, one of whom was her master, Captain Robert Coates. The rest of her crew, including Second Officer William Harland, were picked up by HMS *Acton*.

UB 52 repeatedly attacked the convoy over the next forty-eight hours, claiming another ship, the *Saldanha*, but strangely, little action was taken by the convoy's escorts, not one depth charge being dropped. The convoy reached Gibraltar on 21 March, where a court of enquiry found the escort commander, Lieutenant Commander Connor, 'was, on this occasion, lacking in judgement, initiative, and familiarity with instructions, publications, and procedure'. Connor was relieved of his command. William Harland, on the other hand, remained at sea in merchant ships, eventually gaining command with the Ropner Steamship Company.

Noon sights on 19 October 1939 put the *Rockpool* 350 miles due west of Land's End and within three days' steaming of her destination. Having survived alone this far, her prospects of completing a trouble-free passage were improving with every turn of her screw. It was a beautiful autumn day, the sky clear blue except for a scattering of fair weather cumulus floating like balls of cotton wool, the horizon as sharp as a whetted knife and the sea a serene calm disturbed only by the long swell rolling in from the west. There was not a ship in sight in any direction. It was as if the world had stopped turning. Too quiet for Captain William Harland, who as he left the bridge to go below for his lunch felt decidedly uneasy.

For some reason unable to relax, Harland finished his meal quickly and returned to the bridge, where his fears were suddenly realized. He had no sooner set foot on the scrubbed teakwood deck than the conning tower of a submarine reared up out of the sea about 1½ miles on the starboard beam. Instinctively, Harland ordered the helm hard to port to bring the submarine astern, and as the *Rockpool* answered to the helm, U-48 opened fire with her deck gun. Her first shell fell 100yds short.

Homeward bound U-48 had been running on the surface all night, reeling off the miles at a very satisfying rate, but as she was now approaching British waters, Herbert Schultze had decided to go back to periscope depth at first light. Powered by her electric motors, the U-boat was limited to a frustrating 7½ knots, and when the tall masts and funnel of the *Rockpool* came in sight, Schultze was unable to resist the temptation of sinking just one more enemy ship before the voyage ended. Deep-loaded, slow-moving and unescorted, the British tramp presented an opportunity not to be missed. He gave the order to surface.

By the time the *Rockpool* had steadied up with the U-boat right astern, Colour Sergeant Watkins and his makeshift gun's crew had already reached the after gun platform and had their 4-inch loaded and trained. The gun barked, and their first shell whistled through the air to land within a few feet of U-48's conning tower, throwing up a tall fountain of spray.

And so the running fight began, the *Rockpool*'s long-barrelled 4-inch trading shot for shot with U-48's slightly smaller gun. Below, in the tramp's engine room, bedlam reigned as her engineers coaxed and cajoled her ageing machinery to give its all. The *Rockpool* ran from her aggressor at a never-before-achieved 9 knots, while on her bridge Captain Harland, facing aft, called helm orders as he dodged the fall of shot. His rather laconic report of the action later made to the Admiralty reads:

> At 1235 pm on 19th October in a position 50° 25'N 14° 36'W we sighted a submarine on the starboard beam about 1½ miles away. He opened fire on us firing four shells in quick succession. We put the helm hard aport, and brought him astern. Then we opened fire on him. He dived, and in three or four minutes came up again.
>
> As soon as his periscope came in sight we fired again on him. Every time we bracketed him, and I saw the shells dropping near him and the spray going over his conning tower, he dived.

At 1.45 he was getting his shots too close to us, so I put up a smoke screen and cleared off.

We never saw anything of the submarine but his conning tower. The submarine was using either a six pounder or a 12 pounder. I altered course each time towards the position where the shell fell. The submarine fired about 20 rounds. We fired 13 rounds.

We put over 5 smoke floats, and then I altered course to get in behind the smoke cloud. After putting over the smoke floats, I did not see the submarine again.

The U-boat gave no warning shot, but fired his first four shots in quick succession which passed right over the top of the bridge.

This modest report on the action with U-48 was elaborated on by the *London Gazette* of 15 December 1939, which announced the award of the OBE to Captain William Harland:

A U-boat suddenly appeared on the beam at about one and a half mile's distance, and immediately fired a shot which fell about 100 yards short. The second shot was close on the quarter. The Master at once altered helm to bring the U-boat astern and his gun into action. He fired thirteen rounds, which fell so close that the enemy was drenched with spray. The U-boat fired some twenty rounds, and *Rockpool* was straddled, but not hit. After a stern chase of an hour and a quarter she shook off the enemy by zig-zagging behind a screen of smoke floats. The crew showed great coolness under fire, and all who could helped in the action.

The Master handled his ship in a seamanlike manner and deserves great praise for his coolness and judgement, and for the readiness and efficiency of his ship's company.

It was reported that a British destroyer had arrived in answer to the *Rockpool*'s calls for assistance and had engaged and sunk the U-boat, but this must have been a claim born of wishful thinking. In fact, Herbert Schultze coming to the conclusion that this troublesome British merchantman was best left alone, U-48 left the scene without being further challenged and arrived safely in Kiel on 25 October. She continued to operate against the North Atlantic convoys for more than eighteen months, finally going into retirement in June 1941 having sunk a record fifty-four Allied ships amounting to 311,053 tons gross. As for the *Rockpool*, she suffered no damage during her brush with U-48 and reached the Bristol Channel, docking in Newport, Mon. on 22 October. She survived the war and continued sailing, ending her days in a Japanese breaker's yard in November 1959. Captain William Harland's career, on the other hand, came to a sudden and tragic end in the winter of 1940.

In September 1940 Harland was sent to America to take command of Sir Robert Ropner's latest acquisition, the ex-US Shipping Board's *West Cawthon*, a steamer of 5,912 tons built in California in 1919. The *West Cawthon* had been recently transferred to the Ministry of War Transport under Lend-Lease and handed over to Ropner for management. She was renamed *Empire Bison*.

The *Empire Bison* loaded a cargo of 6,067 tons of scrap metal and ninety-four lorries, some of which were carried on deck, sailing from Baltimore, bound Glasgow, on 19 October. At Halifax she joined forty-three others in Convoy HX 82, which set out to cross the Atlantic on the 20th. The convoy's sole escort for the crossing was the armed merchant cruiser HMS *Alaunia*, an ex-Cunard passenger liner of 14,030 tons.

Soon after leaving Halifax, the paucity of the convoy's escort force became a minor consideration, for the weather deteriorated sharply, and by dawn on the 23rd it was blowing force 9 from the west, with very rough breaking seas and a long heavy swell. With the wind and sea on the quarter, the deep-loaded merchantmen were hard pressed to hold their course, and by noon they were all but hove-to, able to make steerage way only by putting wind and sea on the bow. The *Empire Bison*, in attempting to come about, lost a man overboard, and nothing could be done to save him. Captain Harland regarded this as a bad omen, and he was not surprised when things went from bad to worse.

As the day wore on, the weather showed no improvement, and by nightfall the *Empire Bison* was straggling astern of the convoy in company with four other ships. She soon lost contact with these, and by dawn on the 24th she found herself all alone on a very hostile sea. There now seemed little point in attempting to rejoin the convoy, and as soon as he was able to bring the ship around on to a north-easterly course Harland decided to carry on alone.

There was little change in the weather from then on, but with the wind and sea astern the *Empire Bison* was averaging a steady 9 knots. By 1 November she was some 200 miles north-west of Rockall and just over two days' steaming from the safety of the North Channel. Then she had the misfortune to cross U-124's patrol line.

Two months earlier, U-124, under the command of Kapitän-leutnant Georg-Wilhelm Schultz, had been attacking an east-bound convoy off the Outer Hebrides when she was detected and depth-charged by the Flower-class corvette HMS *Godetia*. Schultz had gone deep to escape but failed to realize that he was in comparatively shallow water. U-124 grounded on the rocky bottom, damaging three of her four bow tubes. Her ability to attack was now very limited, so she was assigned as a weather reporting boat for the remainder of her current patrol.

Schultz sighted the *Empire Bison* during the night of 31 October, and immediately abandoned his weather reporting duties to go on the attack. At about 0700 on 1 November he submerged to periscope depth and fired a single torpedo from his remaining functional bow tube.

The *Empire Bison*, completely unaware that she was being shadowed, was hit on her port side, midway between her No.1 and No.2 holds. To add to the trauma, the torpedo brought the foremast crashing down on to her bridge, and she began to sink at once. In the prevailing weather it was impossible to lower the lifeboats, and so fast did the ship go down that only four men, who were able to launch one of the liferafts, survived. Captain William Harland, who in his short lifetime had survived so much violence, so many crises, died that day, along with thirty of his crew and seven passengers.

CHAPTER SIX

Low Water

In the closing days of 1942, the Battle of the Atlantic, which had been fought with such undying ferocity since the first torpedo was launched in anger three years earlier, was reaching its zenith, and despite the entry of the US Navy into the fray, the German U-boats were gaining the upper hand.

Hitler had finally given in to the persistent lobbying of Admiral Dönitz, and in the last quarter of that year another sixty-nine new boats had been commissioned. When 1943 opened, Dönitz had no fewer than 393 U-boats under his command, of which 212 were operational. This substantial increase in the German Navy's underwater arm, coupled with a spell of exceptionally bad weather in the North Atlantic, had put Britain's vital lifeline to the arsenals and granaries of the Americas in mortal danger of being cut. Then, in March 1943, having realized that Bletchley Park was reading their Enigma-coded messages to the U-boats, German Intelligence added a fourth rotor to their Enigma machines. This was the final straw, leaving the British code-breakers completely blind and giving Dönitz free rein to move his wolf packs into position when a convoy was known to be at sea.

With so many U-boats available for the North Atlantic, the wolf packs were out in force, straddling the convoy lanes, each with often as many as thirty boats stationed 15 to 20 miles apart. Theoretically, any convoy passing through or near any one of these patrol lines would certainly be spotted by at least one of the pack. This boat would then shadow the convoy while calling in the others to mount an attack. It was a situation that spelled disaster for Allied shipping, and with plans for the coming invasion of Sicily and the Italian mainland well under way, more and more convoys were making the perilous voyage from America carrying the guns, ammunition, tanks and supplies needed for the build-up.

It was against this threatening background that Convoy SC 122 sailed from New York on 5 March 1943. SC 122 was a slow convoy of fifty heavily loaded ships, five of which were destined for Iceland, where they would join another convoy to follow the even more perilous route to Arctic Russia. The rest would carry on to various British ports.

The convoy's ocean escort, which joined off Newfoundland, consisted of the British destroyer HMS *Havelock*, the River-class frigate HMS *Swale* and the Flower-class corvettes *Buttercup*, *Godetia*, *Lavender*, *Pimpernel* and *Saxifrage*. With them was the US Navy destroyer USS *Upshur*, which would escort the Arctic convoy ships to Reykjavik, and in support the anti-submarine trawler *Campobello*, then acting as a rescue ship.

Steaming in thirteen columns abreast, and in weather as fair as its gets in the North Atlantic, SC 122 comfortably achieved its designated speed of 7 knots, hardly record-breaking but suited to the sorely overburdened merchantmen, many of which, had it not been for the war, would have been heading for the breaker's yard.

As might have been expected at the approach of the spring equinox, SC 122's honeymoon period was short-lived. Two days out from New York and clear of the Nantucket Shoals, the ships were heading out into the Atlantic proper, when the bottom dropped out of the glass with the arrival of a full gale blowing from the south. With a heavy, tumbling sea on the quarter, and lashed by driving rain squalls, it was not long before the convoy, which had sailed in orderly columns abreast, was scattered far and wide. Unable to hold a sensible course, and in some cases barely able to stay afloat, ships began to drop out of the ranks. Eventually, two put back to New York, and as the nightmare raged on, six more abandoned their voyages and sought shelter in Halifax, Nova Scotia. Fourteen more ships joined from Halifax on the 9th, and with them came the rescue ship *Zamelek*. The arrival of the latter brought new hope to men who lived with the fear that they might soon end up fighting for their lives in the turbulent sea. The reputation of the *Zamelek*, a 1,500-ton ex-Mediterranean trader under the command of Welshman Captain Owen Morris, was paramount. Sailing with Atlantic and Arctic convoys since early 1941, she had picked up more survivors than any other of her class.

This was not an auspicious start to the crossing, and it was becoming ever more fraught with danger as the number of U-boats roaming those waters multiplied day by day. Best estimates were that Dönitz had in the region of 190 front-line boats stalking the North Atlantic convoy lanes. Furthermore, it was unknown to those who sailed in SC 122 – perhaps just as well – that German Intelligence was reading the British merchant ships' codes, was fully aware of the sailing and progress of each convoy and was taking appropriate action.

Three large wolf packs, consisting altogether of forty U-boats, were already setting up an ambush for SC 122. *Grüppe Raubgraf*, ten boats strong, was assembling at the western edge of the Air Gap, the mid-ocean point where Allied aircraft could not reach, while *Grüppe Stürmer*, eighteen boats, and *Grüppe Dränger*, eleven boats, were forming a long patrol line further east.

Six days after SC 122 cleared New York, the fast convoy HX 229 sailed from the same port. Its forty loaded merchantmen, two of which dropped out shortly after sailing, were escorted by the British Escort Group B-4, led by the destroyer HMS *Volunteer*. With her were the ex-US Navy 'four-stackers' HMS *Beverley* and *Mansfield*, plus the Flower-class corvettes *Anemone* and *Pennywort*. Twenty-four hours later, another twenty-eight ships which had been delayed in New York for various reasons left as Convoy HX 229A. They were joined later by sixteen ships from Halifax, while four of the New York ships put into Halifax to await another convoy, as scheduled. When fully assembled, HX 229A consisted of forty Allied ships, with the frigates HMS *Moyola* and *Waveney*, the old sloop HMS *Hastings* and the ex-US Coastguard cutters HMS *Landguard* and *Lulworth* escorting.

Three eastbound Allied convoys were now at sea in close proximity to each other: SC 122 struggling to make 7 knots but rarely succeeding, and the faster HX 229 split into two sections. All told, they made up a huge fleet of 124 ships which, by virtue of their various speeds, were beginning to merge together. German Intelligence, through reading the Allied codes, were aware of this potentially bumper harvest waiting to be reaped and had informed Admiral Dönitz, who then sent in his wolf packs. In the van were the ten boats of *Grüppe Raubgraf*, and racing to support were the eleven of *Grüppe Dränger* and the eighteen of *Grüppe Stürmer*. In addition, Dönitz had called in four other U-boats acting independently in the area. Together, the packs formed an unprecedented strike force of forty-three front-line submarines. The stage was set for a battle of momentous proportions.

As if the dangers the Allied ships faced were not enough, on 15 March SC 122 ran into a violent westerly gale. Despite the mad gyrations of this collection of elderly tramps running before the wind and waves, the storm proved to be a bonus for the convoy, the added speed carrying it past *Grüppe Raubgraf* before its patrol line was set up. However, in the melee the two smallest ships in the convoy, the 755-ton Icelandic-flag *Selfoss* and the anti-submarine trawler *Campobello*, were soon in trouble. The *Selfoss*, fighting a losing battle with the mountainous seas, straggled astern and was eventually lost to sight in the blinding rain and blown spume. By brilliant seamanship, and a great deal of luck, she eventually reached the shelter of Reykjavik. The *Campobello* was less fortunate; she sprang a serious leak in her coal bunkers which could not be stemmed, and was sunk by gunfire on the orders of the Escort Commander.

While SC 122 was safe for the time being, HX 229, following close behind on a similar course, was courting danger. The continuing bad weather had enabled the fast convoy to slip through the *Raubgraf* patrol line unseen on the night of the 15/16th, but it was sighted on the morning of the 16th by U-653. Commanded by Gerhard Feiler, U-653 was low on fuel, had only one torpedo left and had recently lost a man overboard. Not unexpectedly, she had been ordered to return to Biscay.

When Feiler made his chance sighting of Convoy HX 229, he immediately broke radio silence to report to Lorient. Dönitz saw the opportunity for a mass attack and ordered the *Raubgraf* boats to pursue and attack. At the same time, he radioed the twenty-nine boats of *Dränger* and *Stürmer*, instructing them to get ahead of the two other eastbound convoys, HX 229 and HX 229A, and form a line of ambush that could not be bypassed. Meanwhile, all three convoys, SC 122, HX 229 and HX 229A, were drawing ever closer to one another and would eventually form one huge armada of 123 merchant ships, escorted by twenty warships. Covering the ocean as far as the eye could see, this was a sight to be wondered at and a target not to be missed. Dönitz's wolf packs were about to be handed the opportunity of a lifetime.

Grüppe Raubgraf was first to make contact. Hans Joachim Bertelsmann in U-603, ploughing through the breaking seas with his conning tower half awash, sighted and sank the Norwegian motor vessel *Elin K*, the leading ship of Column 10 in HX 229.

The 5,214-ton *Elin K*, commanded by Captain Robert Johannessen, was on a voyage from Australia to Liverpool with 7,000 tons of manganese ore and wheat and had been dogged by bad luck from the outset. Soon after sailing from Sydney at the end of December 1942, she narrowly escaped a Japanese torpedo while crossing the Pacific. Then, nearing the west coast of America, she had run into a storm, during which Boatswain Kristian Kristiansen was washed overboard by a rogue wave and lost. And as if that was not misfortune enough, while in New York awaiting a convoy to cross the Atlantic, the *Elin K* was rammed by the Dutch steamer *Zaanland*, which was waiting for the same convoy. Both ships sustained substantial damage, but after temporary repairs were able to sail with Convoy HX 229 on 11 March.

The *Elin K*'s fate was finally sealed when, shortly after midnight on the 16th, Hans-Joachim Bertelsmann approached HX 229 from the south and fired a spread of four torpedoes. Three of U-603's torpedoes appeared to have missed and gone shooting off into the unknown, but the *Elin K* was the unlucky recipient of the fourth. She was struck on her starboard side in way of her No.4 hold and, dragged down by the deadweight of her ore cargo, immediately began to sink. Fortunately, the corvette *Pennywort* was close by, and Captain Johannessen and his crew of thirty-three were all rescued.

Twenty minutes after U-603 had opened the attack, U-758, with Helmut Manseck in command, joined the battle, again approaching the starboard side of the convoy. As now seemed to be the accepted practice, Manseck fired a spread of four into the heart of the convoy, one of which hit the *Elin K*'s acquaintance from New York harbour, the *Zaanland*, which was carrying refrigerated meat, wheat and zinc from Australia to Avonmouth. Manseck's torpedo ripped open her hull amidships, and she went down in ten minutes. Again, all her crew were picked up by the escorts.

U-758's torpedoes also brought to a premature end the maiden voyage of the American Liberty ship *James Oglethorpe*. Sailing as third ship of Column 9 in HX 229, the *James Oglethorpe* was loaded with 8,000 tons of steel, cotton and food, plus a deck cargo of aircraft, tractors and trucks, all for Liverpool. With the sea flooding in through the hole blown in her No.2 hold, she caught fire and began to settle by the head. Some of her crew abandoned ship without orders, but Captain Albert Long and twenty volunteers stood by their ship and set off to bring her in to St John's, Newfoundland. What happened to her then is not known. Either she sank due to the damage caused by Manseck's torpedo, or some other U-boat came across the wreck and administered the coup de grâce. The ship and Captain Long and his men were never seen again.

Meanwhile, U-338, a *Grüppe Stürmer* boat under the command of Manfred Kinzel located SC 122, then some 120 miles ahead of HX 229. Kinzel manoeuvred into position and at 0005 on the 17th fired two torpedoes from his bow tubes, one of which went home in the hull of the 4,898-ton steamer *Kingsbury*, the leading ship of Column 5. The *Kingsbury*, owned by Alexander Capper of London and commanded by 44-year-old Captain William Laidler, was carrying a cargo of West African produce and 2,000 tons of bauxite from Port Harcourt to London. She sank, taking three crew members and one passenger with her. Fireman Deane Wynne was a survivor:

> I well recall the 17th March. It was St. Patrick's Day, not that I realized that at the time or was even interested in it. It was a date I would remember for the rest of my life though. I came off watch at 8 pm and found it to be a fine and clear night, albeit there was a fair breeze blowing and the seas were still running a bit high from the previous storms. I stood for a while admiring the convoy and getting a bit of fresh air. All seemed quiet and peaceful as I watched the steady roll of our companion ships plodding their weary way home just like us . . . I then went below and turned in. I was soon sound asleep.
>
> A shattering explosion woke me up. The ship gave a great shudder. I looked at my watch, it was 5 minutes past midnight. The throbbing of the engine stopped and the ship took a list to port. I leapt out of my bunk wearing only the underpants I always slept in. I did not wait to grab anything else other than my blue kapok life jacket. I dashed up the ladder on the starboard side and ran along the deck to the lifeboat amidships. It was lucky for me that I chose the starboard side. When I looked back aft from the boat deck, I could see a great gaping hole in the deck on the port side. I would have caught my shins on

the upturned pieces of jagged steel and taken a dive into the hold if I had run down the port side.

By now chaos seemed to be reigning. The stopped engine meant the boiler safety valves were blowing off the high pressure steam with a tremendous noise. We only had two lifeboats, the port side was launched first as the ship was listing that way. The painter rope holding the boat broke as she hit the water and the boat drifted away with one sailor in it, never to be seen again. The ship still had way on her as attempts were made to launch the starboard lifeboat. She got smashed against the ship's side. We looked around for help. There was none. Three other ships had been torpedoed. All four of us were hit within the space of 10 minutes and all by the same U-boat, U-338 . . .

We were the first ship in the seventh column of the convoy, also the first to be torpedoed so we had no warning at all. We watched ships from behind us frantically altering course to avoid collision with us. We were sinking fast. If we were not to be sucked down in the vortex as she sank, or blown up by her boilers, we would have to jump over the side. It took an awful lot of courage to make that jump. It was midnight. We were right in the middle of the North Atlantic, in the middle of March. Thirty foot waves. A sinking ship ready to drag you down with her, and little hope of being picked up. But jump we all did. As I hit the freezing water and went right under it seemed as if I would never reach the surface again. It took an eternity to rise. I was quite surprised when I found myself bobbing on the surface of the water, gasping for breath, and being thrown about by the waves . . .

Deane Wynne and forty-three other survivors from the *Kingsbury* were picked up six hours later by the rescue ship *Zamalek*. Wynne's report continues:

I was taken down to the sick bay where the Royal Navy doctor gave me a quick look over. I was told I would be OK and, no doubt, compared to many of the unfortunates I saw down there, I was. I was then given a large tot of

Navy Rum, wrapped in a blanket, and sat down on the steel deck in the corridor. This was to be my 'perch' for another five days before we got into port. Zamalek had picked up 165 survivors and was grossly overloaded. God only knows what would have happened to us if she was torpedoed with all of us on board.

While Deane Wynne and most of his shipmates took to the water, Captain Laidler, loath to leave his command while she was still afloat, remained aboard the *Kingsbury*. With him were Chief Radio Officer Bertie King and Able Seaman Sam Ward. King had stayed at his post to transmit distress messages, while Ward, who had been at the wheel on the bridge when the torpedo struck, opted to stay with Captain Laidler.

When Laidler reluctantly had to accept that his ship was going down, he sent Ward forward to release one of the liferafts. Unfortunately, the raft broke adrift when it went over the side, and Sam Ward jumped overboard to retrieve it. When in the water, he was hit by a heavy swell that swept him away. The 21-year-old A.B. was never seen again.

Captain Laidler and Radio Officer King had no other option but to go overboard and try to swim to the raft. This they succeeded in doing just as the *Kingsbury* took her last plunge, rearing her bows high in the air and slipping stern first into the deep. Laidler and King were later rescued by the *Zamalek*.

Kinzel's second torpedo hit the ship directly astern of the *Kingsbury*, the 5,072-ton *King Gruffydd*, which was on a voyage from New York to Hull with 5,000 tons of steel, 500 tons of tobacco and 493 tons of high explosives. Commanded by the aptly named Captain Hywel Griffiths, she carried a total complement of forty-nine.

The *King Gruffydd*, built in Hong Kong in 1919 as the *War Trooper*, was a ship with a chequered history. She had been requisitioned by the Admiralty in September 1939 and converted to a Special Service Vessel, being renamed RFA *Maunder*. Some two months later, she was armed with seven 4-inch guns, four Lewis machine guns, four 21-inch torpedo tubes and 100 depth charges, becoming the Q-ship HMS *Maunder*. Her career under the White Ensign was short and largely uneventful, and in September 1941 she was handed over to the Ministry of War Transport, who then appointed

Dodd, Thompson of London to manage her. She became the *King Gruffydd*, just another Welsh tramp.

When Manfred Kinzel's torpedo hit the *King Gruffyd*, breaching her No.1 hold, the 5,000 tons of steel she was carrying began to drag her down at once. There was a rush for the boats, as it was feared that the explosives in the cargo would go up at any minute, but fortunately this did not happen. When Second Officer F. R. Hughes, who had been on the bridge dumping overboard all code books and confidential papers in their weighted bags, reached the boat deck, he found that he and others had been left behind:

> I could see that it was now too late to board the boat by means of the rope ladder as the boat was now well clear of the ship's side and drifting towards the stern of the vessel. The ship had settled further by the head and it was obvious that she was sinking and we had to get clear as soon as possible. I told the others that our only chance was to jump into the water from the after well deck just forward of the poop deck and swim out to intercept the lifeboat as it drifted down. They followed me along the deck but didn't jump into the water after me. They both went down with the ship, as did the captain, who remained on the bridge when I left.
>
> I swam or rather struggled out to the lifeboat which was now about twenty yards from the stricken ship. When I reached the lifeboat I had to hang on to the gunwale while the survivors in the boat rowed it further away from the sinking vessel – they were not about to stop rowing in order to pull me on board. I looked back and saw that the *King Gruffydd* was now lying at an angle of 45 degrees with the propeller and rudder high above the water. Suddenly, as I watched, she dived vertically under the waves.

Encouraged by his initial success, Manfred Kinzel fired another spread of two torpedoes into the massed ranks of the convoy. One missed, but the other hit the *Alderamin*, a Dutch steamer of 7,886 tons on passage from West Africa to Hull with 10,000 tons of oil seeds. Hit squarely amidships, the *Alderamin* broke her back and drifted astern. In an attempt to hasten her demise, Kinzel emptied his stern tube at her, but this torpedo missed and carried on to damage the Canadian-built *Fort Cedar Lake* in the adjacent column. She also dropped astern and nine hours later fell victim to torpedoes from U-665.

It now seemed that SC 122 had slipped from the enemy's grasp and was free to continue to the east, but this was not to be. Lacking intelligence as a result of the change in the German naval codes, the Admiralty was not aware that two more wolf packs, *Dränger* and *Stürmer*, twenty-nine U-boats in all, were to the east and waiting for the slow convoy to sail into their trap.

An hour passed, and all that could be heard was the crash of the waves against the bulwarks of the labouring ships and the howl of the storm-force wind. Otherwise, the quiet of the night was almost uncanny. There were those who dared to whisper, 'They've gone away', and there was a noticeable slackening of the built-up tension. Cups of hot cocoa were passed around and illicit cigarettes lit in sheltered corners.

It was a false dawn. The U-boats had been below reloading their tubes, and at 2230 Siegfried Stretlow in U-435 approached the starboard side of the convoy unseen and fired a spread of two torpedoes at the outer ranks. These raced through a gap in the outer column, homing in on the 7,196-ton American Liberty *William Eustis*, second ship of Column 2. One torpedo narrowly missed her stern, but the other hit forward of her bridge. She went down by the head, slowly and gracefully, taking 7,000 tons of Cuban sugar with her. Her crew were picked up four hours later by HMS *Volunteer*.

Soon after midnight, Heinz Walkerling in U-91 followed Stretlow in, again approaching from the south and firing five torpedoes in quick succession at the shadowy outlines of the merchantmen. Only one found its mark.

The outside column of any convoy is always a dangerous position to be occupying, more especially when you are leading that column, as was another American Liberty, the *Harry Luckenbach*. During the preceding daylight hours Captain Ralph McKinnon had made his protest by breaking ranks and zig-zagging at speed ahead of the convoy, but he had been quickly ushered back into line by the escorts. When one of Heinz Walkerling's torpedoes slammed into the *Harry Luckenbach*'s engine room, Captain McKinnon had only the fleeting satisfaction of knowing that his fears had been well founded.. Three minutes later, the *Harry Luckenbach* and her cargo of war supplies had gone to the bottom. McKinnon and his crew of seventy-nine abandoned ship in three boats, but all three disappeared into the night, never to be seen again.

For a while, HX 229's escorts chased their tails in the darkness, hurling depth charges in all directions, but to no avail. The wily U-boats had again withdrawn. There were those in the convoy who now feared they would not see another dawn, and they had good reason. The grey wolves chose the graveyard hours to make their return, Bernhard Zurmühlen in U-600 slipping through the escort screen at 0300 to empty his bow tubes at the starboard column. The four torpedoes streaked past the outer ships to find targets deep in the convoy.

The 8,714-ton British steamer *Nariva* was the first victim, brought to a sudden halt with a hit amidships. Upright, but visibly lower in the water, she dropped out of the ranks and drifted astern. Minutes later, she was followed by the 12,156-ton British ex-whale factory ship *Southern Princess*, loaded with 10,053 tons of heavy fuel oil and a deck cargo of locomotives and landing craft. She caught fire and drifted astern, a giant flaming torch lighting up the night.

Zurmühlen's third victim was the American steamer *Irenée Du Pont*, bound from New York to Liverpool and down to her marks with 5,800 tons of general in her holds and a deck cargo of 3,200 tons of oil in drums, topped off with eleven bomber aircraft. Crippled, she fell astern with the others. Ironically, her master, Captain Simonson, had earlier in the day requested of the Commodore that as a 16-knot vessel the *Ireneé Du Pont* be allowed to leave the convoy and go on alone at full speed. His request was, of course, refused. Later in the day, the *Ireneé Du Pont* was given the coup de grâce by U-91, along with the *James Oglethorpe*, *William Eustis* and *Nariva*, all of which had been abandoned by their crews and were forming a ghost convoy astern of HX 229.

Dawn came and went on the 17th with only a faint paling of the heavily overcast sky. The wind and sea were undiminished in their ferocity, but the intrepid Hans-Achim von Rosenberg-Gruszcynski in U-384 made a stealthy approach to the starboard column of HX 229 and at 1105 launched a spread of three torpedoes. Rosenberg-Gruszcynski claimed to have sunk two ships and damaged another. In fact, his torpedoes sank only the British refrigerated ship *Coracero*, on her way from Buenos Aires to Liverpool with 5,758 tons of meat and a large quantity of mail. Despite the weather, only five of her crew were lost.

While U-384 was attacking, Jürgen Krüger in U-631 also made his approach and fired another spread of three at the Allied ships. Again, only one ship was hit. She was the Dutch-flag ex-German steamer *Terkoelei*, bound from Australian ports to Swansea with a full cargo of zinc and wheat. In an ensuing panic on the part of some of her Lascar crew, two lifeboats were dragged down when the ship capsized. Thirty-six men lost their lives.

While HX 229 was under attack, the nearby SC 122 was also having to defend herself. U-338 had slipped through the screen on the northern side of the convoy, and Manfred Kinzel had added to the chaos with a spread of four from his bow tubes. The only ship unfortunate enough to be hit was the US-owned, Panama-flag *Granville*, carrying a cargo of arms for Russia via Iceland. Her voyage came to a sudden end as she plunged to the bottom, taking thirteen of her crew and her generously donated cargo with her.

At the height of this battle, and within earshot of the crashing torpedoes and thumping depth charges, Convoy 229A, the thirty-four ships delayed from sailing with HX 229, sailed past undetected by the enemy. They reached Liverpool nine days later, with one sad exception. On 19 March, when 70 miles south of Cape Farewell, the 14,795-ton *Svend Foyn*, a Norwegian tanker sailing under British colours, hit an iceberg in fog and foundered two days later, with the loss of forty-three lives.

By the time darkness closed in on the 17th, HX 229 had overtaken SC 122, and the two convoys were merging into one huge armada. With so many targets within their grasp, the U-boats attacked with new vigour. At 2014 Rudolf Bahr in U-305 had the British refrigerated ship *Port Auckland* in his sights. He snapped off two torpedoes, one of which went home in the latter's engine room, bringing her to an abrupt halt. She sank later in the night, and another 7,000 tons of frozen Australian lamb ended up on the ocean floor.

Bahr's second torpedo also found a target, the 4,256-ton *Zouave*, a British steamer en route from West Africa to Middlesbrough with 7,100 tons of iron ore. With her hull breached, the great weight of her cargo took her down in less than five minutes. Thirteen men died with her.

The combined escort force now put up such a spirited defence that the U-boats were forced to pull back, and it was early afternoon on the 18th before they returned to the attack, Hans-Hartwig Trojer in U-221 picking off the US Liberty ship *Walter Q. Gresham* with a stern shot. Thus ended another brave maiden voyage, with 10,000 tons of sorely needed foodstuffs denied to hard-pressed Britain. Twenty-eight men died when their lifeboat capsized in heavy seas.

Six minutes after dealing the death blow to the *Walter Q. Gresham*, Trojer aimed another three torpedoes into the massed convoys, two of which hit the 8,293-ton British motor vessel *Canadian Star*, condemning a further 8,000 tons of frozen meat, cheese and butter to the bottom. The weather was now, if anything, worse, and a lifeboat and several rafts were swamped by heavy seas as the crew abandoned ship. Twenty-five men were lost.

When darkness fell, deterred partly by the weather but mostly by the need to regroup and reload, the U-boats withdrew, returning again in the early hours of the 19th.

At long last the curtain was rung down on the massacre of the convoys by Herbert Stengel in the conning tower of U-666. He fired a random spread of three, one of which hit the Greek steamer *Carras*, bound from Rosario to Belfast with a full cargo of bulk wheat. Although listing heavily, the Greek was still afloat when Stengel found her again late that night and administered the coup de grâce.

The surviving ships were now some 300 miles south of Iceland, and help was at hand. The combined escorts were reinforced by the arrival of the American destroyer USS *Babbitt* from Reykjavik and the British destroyer HMS *Highlander*, accompanied by the Flower-class corvette *Abelia*, from Northern Ireland. Air cover was also provided by Coastal Command VLR Liberators from Iceland and Aldergrove. It was one of these aircraft that sighted and sank U-384, consigning Hans-Achim von Rosenberg-Gruszczynski and all his crew to the deep. This was the signal for Dönitz to call off his wolves.

The running battle for the three eastbound convoys had lasted three days and three nights and had involved 122 merchant ships, twenty-one escorts, and an attacking force of forty-four U-boats. It was a clash of arms unprecedented in the annals of the Battle of the Atlantic, resulting in the loss of twenty-two merchantmen and their cargoes, along with more than 300 merchant seamen. Berlin's propaganda machine went into top gear, claiming thirty-two Allied ships and 186,000 tons of cargo destroyed, 'the greatest ever success against any convoy'. An exaggeration typical of the B-Dienst perhaps, but the loss of so many ships, so much cargo and so many brave men was seen in London as a major setback. And this was at a time when Britain was already suffering severe shortages of food, fuel and war materials from across the Atlantic, fuel supplies being particularly low. After nearly four years of bloody and unrelenting war, the spectre of defeat was again beginning to show its fearful head. What happened in the North Atlantic in the coming months would decide the issue once and for all.

PART TWO
The Turn of the Tide

CHAPTER SEVEN

Evening Departure

The North Channel was in a sombre mood when, in the early afternoon of Thursday, 22 April 1943, Convoy ONS 5 began to assemble for the Atlantic crossing. The sky, already heavily overcast, was lowering ominously, while even in these relative sheltered waters between Ireland and Scotland the swell had assumed a threatening heave, and curtains of drizzly rain were drawing across the horizon in the west. In the gathering gloom the tall headlands of the island of Islay were still visible to starboard, but they were fading fast. Those who had been this way before sniffed the wind and shook their heads. Something nasty was brewing out there in the wild Atlantic.

The ships had come from all points of the compass, from the Bristol Channel, from Liverpool, from the Clyde and from nearby Londonderry. They were a mixed bunch, thirty flying the Red Ensign, four under the Stars and Stripes and one Panamanian; then there were the exiles: two Dutch, one Danish, one Greek, one Polish and even a Yugoslav. Most were rust-streaked and rather elderly, and all flying light in ballast, with the exception of the seven Bristol Channel ships which carried token cargoes of 'Best Welsh' for the coaling station at St John's, and the two tankers, one British and one American, deep-loaded with bunker oil to service the escorts. All without exception were veterans of the North Atlantic convoy run and fully aware of the dangers awaiting them. Two of their number, Blue Funnel Line's *Dolius* and the US-flag *McKeesport*, were survivors of the terrible mauling meted out to HX 229 and SC 122 by a U-boat pack just a month earlier. That they were back for more illustrated the sheer determination of Allied merchant seamen not to be cowed by the enemy. But for the most part they were career seamen, and in their view they were merely carrying on doing the only job they knew. The U-boats were just another added danger.

There was no man in the convoy more aware of the huge odds they faced than 21-year-old Third Officer William Skinner,

then busy with flag signals on the bridge of J. & C. Harrison's
5,081-ton steamer *Harbury*. In his four short years at sea young Bill
Skinner had stared death in the face all too often, beginning with
his first ship, the *Hardingham*, which he had joined as a fresh-faced
cadet in 1939. Just six months later, in the early summer of 1940,
the 5,415-ton *Hardingham* had been blown from under him by a
German mine in the North Sea. It had been a brutal introduction
to the war, but one which Skinner survived with nothing more
than a few bruises and a thorough wetting.

Two years later, Skinner, elevated to the rank of Third Officer
by the casualties of war, was serving aboard another of Harrison's,
the 5,082-ton *Harpasa*, in the Indian Ocean. Japan was now in the
war, but her influence had not yet been felt this far west, and
the *Harpasa* was in waters regarded as relatively safe. Then, on
31 March 1942, reports were received that Admiral Nagumo's
fleet of battleships and aircraft carriers was heading for Ceylon.
Invasion seemed likely, and the Admiralty ordered all Allied
merchant ships in India's west coast ports to put to sea and run for
the safety of ports in East Africa to avoid capture.

Most of the escaping ships formed unescorted convoys, more
for peace of mind than protection. The *Harpasa*, however, sailed
alone, leaving Calcutta on the morning of 1 April with orders to
make for Mombasa, where the British Eastern Fleet was now based.
Being a fairly new ship, the *Harpasa* was capable of a good turn of
speed, and for the first forty-eight hours at sea, with no sign of the
Japanese fleet, it seemed that she would get away unmolested.

Easter Sunday dawned with the horizon still empty except for
the occasional dhow, and Captain Atkinson was quietly congratulating himself on having escaped the clutches of the enemy, when
an aircraft clearly identified as Japanese by its Rising Sun mark-
ings suddenly dropped out of the clouds. The plane, from one of
Nagumo's carriers, roared over the ship and dropped a stick of
bombs, several of which fell on the *Harpasa*'s after deck. Six of her
crew were killed outright, and the ship was soon burning furi-
ously and sinking. Her remaining crew fought hard to save her,
but their efforts were in vain. Some hours later, Atkinson gave the
order to abandon ship. Luckily for the survivors, Third Officer
Bill Skinner among them, the British ship *Taksang*, which had left
Calcutta after the *Harpasa*, was following in her wake, and they
were picked up within hours.

Skinner's ordeal did not end there. Next morning, the *Taksang* had joined up with seven other ships in an improvised convoy when they were overhauled by Admiral Nagumo's squadron. The *Taksang* made an effort to escape, working up to a speed in excess of 18 knots, but she came under heavy fire from the Japanese cruisers. Her bridge took the full force of the attack, her master, Captain Costello, being gravely wounded. Fifteen others, including First Radio Officer Alfred Child of the *Harpasa*, were killed by the first enemy salvo.

Minutes later, the *Taksang*, battered and on fire from stem to stern, capsized and sank. The survivors of both ships' crews, many with serious shrapnel wounds, got away in two lifeboats and a raft. They were picked up after two days adrift by another Allied ship.

These harrowing memories were fresh in Bill Skinner's mind as he made preparations for the coming Atlantic crossing. In four short years he had gone from boy to man and learned the hard lesson that going to sea in a merchant ship in time of war was an extremely hazardous undertaking.

Night was drawing in before the forty-three merchantmen making up Convoy ONS 5 were formed up, and the only land still visible was the American monument on Islay to two troopships lost with many lives in the 1914–1918 war. Standing tall, so that it seemed almost to touch the low overcast, the tower stood like a warning finger to those about to challenge the broad Atlantic.

The tragic events that resulted in the American war memorial on Islay began with the *Tuscania*, a 14,348-ton passenger liner of the Glasgow-based Anchor Line. A Clyde-built ship launched in September 1914, the *Tuscania* ran a luxury passenger service between New York and Glasgow, until she was requisitioned by the Admiralty in 1916 and converted to a troopship.

On 24 January 1918 the *Tuscania* sailed from New York with 2,013 US troops on board, bound for Liverpool. Once at sea, she joined a convoy which crossed the Atlantic unmolested; but on the morning of 5 February, as the ships approached the North Channel, they were sighted by Korvettenkapitän Wilhelm Meyer in the German submarine U-77. Meyer shadowed the convoy during the hours of daylight, surfacing as soon as it was dark. The *Tuscania*, being the largest and most prominent ship in the convoy, became the target of Meyer's first torpedoes. He fired two, one of which missed, but the other blasted a hole in the *Tuscania's* hull below the waterline. Fortunately, the trooper remained afloat for another four hours before sinking, allowing the British destroyers *Mosquito* and *Pigeon* to take off most of her passengers and crew. A total of 230 men lost their lives, of whom 201 were believed to be American servicemen.

The 12,124-ton *Otranto*, of the Orient Line, began her wartime career in 1914 as an armed merchant cruiser. She spent much of the war in the South Atlantic, but in late 1918 when the demand for ferrying American troops across the North Atlantic became more urgent, the *Otranto* joined the ranks of British ex-passenger ships to be converted to trooping.

When the *Otranto* sailed from New York on 25 September 1918 she was appointed Commodore ship of Convoy HX 50 and had on board a detachment of 358 American servicemen, bound for France via Liverpool. Six days out from New York, on the Grand Banks of Newfoundland, the convoy ran into a patch of dense fog, with visibility down to a few yards. In the ensuing melee the *Otranto* collided with, and sank, the French fishing schooner *Croisine*. The liner suffered little damage, except that some of her lifeboats were smashed in their davits.

Three days later, the weather began to deteriorate as a depression moved in from the west, and when dawn broke on 5 October it was blowing force 11, with mountainous seas. The convoy was now approaching the north coast of Ireland and due to rendezvous with an escort of British destroyers. Unfortunately, the wind was then so ferocious that the destroyers were unable to leave port, and its ocean escort having already detached to another convoy, HX 50 was left to fend for itself.

With the wind ratcheting up to near-hurricane force, and visibility seriously reduced by rain and flying spume, the tight discipline of the convoy began to give way to confusion. There had been no sun or star observations for some days, navigation being solely by dead reckoning, which in waters where tides and currents are often unpredictable was liable to be woefully inaccurate. This being an age when there was no other accurate means of position-fixing, it is fair to say that HX 50 was hopelessly lost.

In the midst of all this chaos the *Otranto* was in collision for the second time in the crossing. She was rammed by another

British trooper, the *Kashmir*, which in the general confusion ran headlong into her port side near her engine room. The *Otranto* was holed from her waterline to her main deck, and both boiler rooms, then her engine room, were flooded. Engineless and listing heavily to port, she drifted slowly on to the jagged rocks of Islay. Before she grounded, in spite of the shrieking wind and angry seas, the destroyer HMS *Mounsey* went alongside the doomed ship and took off 300 US troops, 266 of the liner's crew and thirty of the crew of the French schooner *Croisine*, who had lost their ship only days earlier. Such was the ferocity of the pounding seas that within twenty-four hours all that remained of the *Otranto* was a pile of broken steel. It was never established exactly how many men died with the trooper, but it is estimated to have been at least 470, of whom some 358 were American servicemen. When war came along again twenty-one years later, the tall stone tower on Islay was all that remained to tell of the sacrifice made by those men.

Appointed as Convoy Commodore for ONS 5 was 54-year-old Acting Commodore James Kenneth Brook DSO, RNR, who was no newcomer to ships and the sea. An ex-merchant seaman, he had served in the last of the square-riggers at the turn of the century, and as a reservist had commanded 'Q' ships in the 1914–1918 war, being awarded the DSO for sinking a German U-boat when commanding HMS *Privet*. Between the wars he had been in command of cargo liners trading to the Far East, and although officially retired, had returned to sea in 1940 to join the growing band of Convoy Commodores. His mettle had already been tested when sailing in the former French tanker *President Sergent*, torpedoed off Cape Farewell in November 1942.

The *President Sergent*, a 5,344-ton oil tanker of the Anglo Saxon Petroleum Company, with Captain Brook aboard as Convoy Commodore, was sailing at the head of Convoy ONS 144, bound from New York to Liverpool. At about 0600 on 18 November 1942, without warning, a torpedo slammed into the British tanker's hull, and she began to settle in the water. She did not sink, however, and about three and a half hours later, the same U-boat found her drifting with a heavy list and very deep in the water. The U-boat duly delivered the coup de grâce, and the *President Sergent* went down, taking twenty of her crew with her. Commodore Brook and his staff of six, along with the tanker's master and twenty-three of his crew, were picked up by the rescue ship *Perth*.

Fully blooded in both World Wars, James Kenneth Brook was amply qualified to see ONS 5 safely through the dangers it faced in the Atlantic's deep waters.

Brook and his staff of signallers were accommodated in the 5,242-ton Norwegian motor vessel *Rena*, which was under the command of Captain Finn Salvesen. She was one of the 'Free Norwegian Fleet', ships that had escaped capture by the Germans when Norway fell in April 1940. At that time she had been on her way from Hampton Roads to Trinidad, and Captain Salvesen had taken her to the nearest British port and offered his services to the Admiralty. The *Rena* had been part of the North Atlantic convoy scene ever since.

How the *Rena* came to be chosen as Commodore ship for ONS 5 is not on record, but in hindsight, of all the ships in the convoy she was possibly the least suited to that exalted role. She was neither young nor fast, dating from 1924; moreover, like all Norwegian merchantmen, she was 'dry', and Commodore Brook would have to forgo his customary tot of whisky. Her only apparent asset was that, being an ex-cargo/passenger ship, she did have ample spare accommodation.

By the time Commodore Brook had coaxed his assortment of tramps and cargo liners into convoy order, twelve columns abreast, with three or four ships to each column, the island of Islay was only a dark smudge on the horizon astern. The flashing light on Oversay, functioning on low power, was barely able to pierce the gloom.

Brook had stationed the *Rena* at the head of Column 6. To port of her was the British motor vessel *Losada*, and to starboard the ex-German, now British-flag *Empire Advocate*. Directly astern of the *Rena* were the two fleet oilers, the USS *Argon* and the *British Lady*, safely tucked up in the heart of the convoy and hopefully protected from the enemy's torpedoes by the other ships. The outriders of ONS 5, on the four corners of the convoy, were another four British ships, namely the *Bristol City* leading Column 1, *Empire Planet* leading Column 12, *Dunsley* bringing up the rear of the same column, and *Temple Arch*, rear ship of Column 1. These ships had no official role, but their masters were all experienced men who would be expected to keep any stragglers in line.

Above: The 4-inch Mk.VII anti-submarine gun. (*Awesome Ocean*)

Below: The American monument on Islay. (*Islayinfo.com*)

Above: The Norwegian collier *Bonde*. (*Markus Berger*)

Below: French 'supertanker' *Emile Miguet*. (*Musee Portuaire*)

Above: Escort depth charging Asdic contact. (*IWM*)

Below: Harrison Line's *Harbury*. (*Library of Contemporary History, Stuttgart*)

Above: A Hedgehog pattern explodes astern. (*US Coastguard*)

Below: A Hedgehog anti-submarine mortar. (*Royal Navy Official Photographer*)

Right: Kapitänleutnant Herbert Schultze.
(*Deutsches Wehrkundarchiv*)

Below: The Ropner Line's *Heronspool*.
(*Ropner & Co.*)

Above: HMS *Pink*. (*Flower-class Corvette Forum*)

Below: The North Atlantic aroused. (*Doc Vernon*)

Above: The French submarine *Surcouf*. (*Michael de Villier*)

Below: A merchant ship's gun's crew, 1940. (*Source unknown*)

Above: U-48 returns to Kiel after a successful patrol. (*Source unknown*)

Below: Admiral Dönitz congratulating German U-boat sailors after their victorious return. (*Source unknown*)

When fully assembled, Convoy ONS 5 covered an area of some six square miles, the size of a substantial city on shore. Unavoidably, as there were many elderly steamers in the ranks, the convoy's presence was well advertised by a persistent pall of black smoke hanging overhead and visible for many miles.

ONS 5's escort for the ocean passage was Escort Group B-7, under the command of Commander Peter Gretton RN. Charged with the protection of forty-three merchant ships were the destroyer *Duncan*, in which Gretton, the Senior Officer Escort, sailed, the River-class frigate *Tay* (Lieutenant Commander Robert Sherwood RNR), the four Flower-class corvettes *Loosestrife* (Lieutenant Herbert Stonehouse RNR), *Pink* (Lieutenant Robert Atkinson DSC, RNR), *Snowflake* (Lieutenant Harold Chesterman RNR) and *Sunflower* (Acting Lieutenant Commander James Plomer RCNVR). In support were the two anti-submarine trawlers *Northern Gem* and *Northern Spray*, who were also to act as rescue ships.

Although small in number, Group B-7 had been honed into a highly effective fighting force by Commander Gretton. Joining the Royal Navy at an early age as a cadet at Dartmouth, between the wars Gretton had served in the aircraft carrier *Courageous*, and later saw action in the cruiser *Durban* during Mussolini's Abyssinian adventure, and in the Spanish Civil War. During these years he had found time to train as a pilot and complete an anti-submarine course at Portsmouth. When war broke out, he was serving as First Lieutenant in the destroyer *Vega* and later joined HMS *Cossack* in the same rank. In *Cossack* Gretton fought at the Second Battle of Narvik, before being appointed to command the destroyer *Sabre*, on which he cut his teeth in the North Atlantic convoys. Promotion to Lieutenant Commander came in June 1942, and he took command of the destroyer *Wolverine*. In her he was involved in Operation Pedestal, which resulted in the relief of Malta, and distinguished himself by ramming and sinking the Italian submarine *Dagabur*. In December 1942 he was promoted to Commander and appointed as Senior Officer Escort of Group B-7, sailing in HMS *Duncan*. Along the way, Peter Gretton had collected the Distinguished Service Cross, a Mention in Despatches, the Order of the British Empire and the Distinguished Service Order, the latter awarded for his work in Operation Pedestal.

HMS *Duncan*, a D-class destroyer commissioned in 1933, had seen service with Admiral Somerville's Eastern Fleet in the Indian Ocean, before returning home in late 1942 to refit as a convoy escort leader. When Gretton joined her in March 1943, her 'A' gun had been replaced by a Hedgehog forward-throwing mortar with twenty-four barrels, each firing a 65lb shell designed to explode on impact. She had also been equipped with Type 271 Radar, but for all her new assets she still suffered from a severe handicap in that her twin Parsons geared steam turbines had a voracious appetite for fuel oil. This was a constant source of worry for Commander Gretton, prompting him to station *Duncan* in the centre of the convoy, two ships astern of the *Rena*, Commodore Brook's ship, and flanked by the Cardiff tramp *Campus* to port and Andrew Weir's *Baron Elgin* to starboard. Thus placed, *Duncan* would be able to amble along at the convoy's speed of 7½ knots for much of the time and so save fuel, but still be ready for a high-speed dash should the need arise. The frigate *Tay* he stationed ahead, while the four corvettes covered the flanks of the convoy. The anti-submarine trawlers *Northern Gem* and *Northern Spray* brought up the rear. It was a poor compromise, but the best on offer.

Commander Gretton had already discounted using the *Argon* for refuelling his escorts, as she used the American method of side-by-side refuelling, which involved a high risk of collision, especially in the weather expected in the Atlantic. He favoured the *British Lady*, which was equipped with buoyant rubber hoses which she streamed astern for the escort to pick up.

'Oil could be pumped through the hose at a reasonable rate, and once secured the operation did not take very long', Gretton noted, 'perhaps two hours for a normal refuel. But picking up the gear was not easy, especially in bad weather, and station keeping astern of the tanker was a difficult task.'

Gretton and the *British Lady* were no strangers, having worked together in the ill-fated Norwegian campaign of 1940, and prior to joining Convoy ONS 5 *Duncan* and the tanker had practised refuelling at sea. The *British Lady*, which had played a significant part in Norway, was unusual for a fleet oiler in that she was still under the Red Ensign and manned by merchant seamen. She had been requisitioned by the Admiralty in October 1939 but remained under the management of the British Tanker Company.

While based in Londonderry, Gretton had worked up B-7 to a peak of efficiency, with special emphasis on the use of the High Frequency Direction Finder, so that the Group were especially adept at obtaining cross-bearings on any U-boat transmitting in the vicinity. German U-boat commanders were notorious gossips, using their radios with careless abandon to chat to other boats and communicate with Lorient. Gretton also exercised his ships remorselessly in Asdic and depth charge drills, so that B-7 soon became a force to be reckoned with.

The Group had returned to Londonderry just over a week earlier after escorting the fast convoy HX 231 from New York. This was a large convoy of sixty-seven loaded ships, including twenty-two tankers, routed to the north and passing within 300 miles of Iceland. Gretton, sailing in the frigate *Tay*, had with him the destroyer *Vidette* and the corvettes *Alisma*, *Pink*, *Snowflake* and *Loosestrife*.

For the most part, the weather was atrocious, and station-keeping had proved to be nigh-on impossible. However, despite a full head-gale and heavy seas, the convoy was able to maintain an average speed of 10½ knots. Then, despite some air support from Iceland, the convoy when 450 miles south of Cape Farewell was attacked by a pack of eleven U-boats. There followed a fierce running fight in which six of the merchant ships, totalling 77,000 tons gross, and over 200 men had been lost. Gretton's ships put up a magnificent defence, sinking two U-boats and so badly damaging four others that they were forced to retire from the fight. The action was seen as a feather in Gretton's cap, but he had no wish to repeat it with ONS 5.

ONS 5 was routed even further to the north than HX 231, and in addition to the inevitable foul weather was liable to run into pack ice. Gretton was aware that the U-boats would suffer equally and knew that a number of eastbound convoys were due to pass to the south at the same time, which he hoped would prove something of a distraction. In fact, when ONS 5 left the North Channel to begin her Atlantic crossing, five eastbound convoys were also at sea, all loaded to the gunwales with war materials destined for British ports in preparation for the invasion of continental Europe, then expected in the spring of 1944. There were also three other convoys westbound ahead of ONS 5 heading for North America to pick up similar cargoes. In all, when ONS 5 set out for Halifax, a total of 350 Allied merchantmen were at sea in the North Atlantic. Dönitz's U-boats would have no shortage of targets, and Gretton's collection of elderly, largely empty ships would hardly be worth a second glance.

Seasoned escort commander though Peter Gretton might be, he was unable to second guess the German Admiral, who for some reason unknown seemed determined to ambush and smash the Halifax-bound Convoy ONS 4, forty-two ships which sailed from Liverpool nine days before ONS 5. Dönitz had called in no fewer than fifty-eight of his U-boats, probably most of those at sea in the North Atlantic at the time, and set up three patrol lines designed to catch ONS 4 as it crossed. They consisted of Group *Specht* (Woodpecker), a line of seventeen boats lying in wait to the south of Greenland, Group *Meise* (Blue tit), thirty boats in an east-west line in the eastern approaches to Greenland, and Group *Amsel* (Blackbird), eleven boats in a similar line further south.

Even Karl Dönitz was not infallible, however, and despite his meticulous planning, ONS 4 slipped past his nets unseen. This left ONS 5 heading straight into a spider's web from which there could be no escape. And this was at a time when a fourth rotor had unexpectedly been added to the German Enigma, and Bletchley Park was temporarily unable to read the U-boats' radio traffic. Neither the Admiralty, nor Commander Peter Gretton, Commodore James Brook or anyone else concerned with ONS 5 was aware of the grave danger threatening the convoy.

Once clear of Malin Head, Ireland's most northerly point, ONS 5 headed out into the open Atlantic in the teeth of a rising gale. The route as laid down by the Admiralty was north-westerly for 300 miles, then due west to Cape Farewell, then a short leg south-westwards to Halifax. The total distance to steam was 2,800 miles. The voyage would offer little comfort, for reaching so far north would involve freezing temperatures, perhaps pack ice and, at the best, storm force winds and high seas; but if all this meant avoiding the U-boats, then it would be worth the discomfort.

Perversely, things started to go wrong right from the outset. The convoy was not long out of sight of the land when the 37-year-old Polish ship *Modlin*, bringing up the rear of Column 8, signalled that she had serious engine problems and would have to put back to the Clyde. ONS 5 had lost its first ship without a shot being fired.

The remainder of the convoy carried on in rapidly deteriorating weather. The wind had begun to keen ominously in the
rigging, and flecks of phosphorescent spray were whipping over
the bulwarks of the merchantmen as they dug their blunt bows
into the rising seas. By dawn on the 23rd which was little more
than a paling of the heavy overcast, it was blowing a full gale
from the west. The optimistic convoy speed of 7½ knots became
a travesty as the ballasted ships struggled to maintain even
steerage way.

By noon Gretton had become concerned about the amount of oil
Duncan was consuming as the slim-built warship fought to make
headway against the rising seas, and he decided that, in spite of
the weather, he would be wise to top up his tanks from the fleet
oiler *British Lady*. Both ships dropped astern and manoeuvred into
position, with the tanker leading and trailing her reinforced bunkering hose astern for *Duncan* to pick up. The destroyer, following close astern, succeeded in getting the hose aboard, but within
minutes of commencing the transfer of fuel the hose broke adrift
in the heavy seas. Several more attempts were made, but with the
same disastrous result. In the end, Gretton was forced to admit
that refuelling his ship at sea was not possible unless the weather
improved – and that seemed most unlikely. The other oiler, the
American tanker *Argon*, had canvas bunker hoses and could only
refuel ships that came alongside her, a procedure that was clearly
out of the question in the weather prevailing.

By this time *Duncan's* tanks were seriously low, and being unable
to refuel within the foreseeable future, her ability to function to
her full capacity was in question. B-7 without its leading ship able
to make high-speed dashes and use her sub-killing Hedgehog
to good effect was a sorely weakened escort force. Meanwhile,
Gretton used *Duncan* and the frigate *Tay* to make occasional
sweeps ahead of the convoy, using their Asdic and radar to seek
out any U-boats that might be lying in wait for the convoy. The
two ships could detect no alien presence but, unknown to them,
one U-boat, equally unaware of the approach of the convoy, was
just out of sight over the horizon ahead.

U-710, a Type VIIC, was on her maiden war patrol and in
deep waters for the first time, having spent seven months since
commissioning with a training flotilla in the Baltic. Her commander, Oberleutnant zur See Dietrich von Carlewitz, was equally

inexperienced, despite having served in the Kriegsmarine since 1936. He had spent the first nine months as a technical officer in the heavy cruiser *Admiral Scheer*, but thereafter had held posts in various shore establishments and had seen little of the sea. In early September 1943 he had been given command of the new-ly-launched U-710, and after spending several more months in the Baltic working her up had been ordered to join the other boats currently harassing Allied shipping in the North Atlantic.

U-710 sailed from Kiel on 15 April 1943, called at Kristiansand in occupied Norway for fuel, and entered the North Sea on the 17th. She encountered fine but blustery weather, which prevailed while she rounded Shetland and passed between the Faroes and Iceland. This proved to be a difficult passage for von Carlewitz and his newly-trained crew, for in the daylight hours British and American aircraft, handily based in Iceland and the Outer Hebrides, always seemed to be overhead. This forced U-710 to spend most of the day running submerged, coming to the surface only at night.

Commander Gretton first learned of the presence of the enemy when he received a radio message from a B-17 Flying Fortress of 206 Squadron RAF Coastal Command flown by Flying Officer Cowley. The aircraft, on anti-submarine patrol from the Outer Hebrides, had surprised U-710 on the surface, and instead of crash-diving, the inexperienced von Carlewitz had ordered the U-boat's twin C/30 anti-aircraft guns to be manned. Inaccurate fire from her .79-inch guns did nothing to deter the Fortress, which came roaring in and straddled the submarine with depth charges. Her pressure hull was blasted open and she began to sink, then Cowley completed the kill by dropping a second pattern of charges on the wreckage. U-710's first war patrol had lasted just 24 days. She went to the bottom taking Oberleutnant Dietrich von Carlewitz and his crew of forty-eight with her.

CHAPTER EIGHT

The Attack Begins

At sunset on the 25th, ONS 5 was 120 miles west of the lonely island of Rockall, deep into the Atlantic proper, and was all but hove to by a storm-force west-north-westerly wind. The columns of the convoy were in complete disarray, each ship intent on fighting its own lonely battle against the mountainous seas rolling in from the west. Commodore Brook was doing his level best with signal lamp and flags to maintain some semblance of control, but the reins were slipping from his grasp. He could already count seven ships showing two red lights vertical, indicating that they were no longer under command, and there would be more to come.

As darkness closed in, with forty-two ships without lights attempting to steam in close proximity to each other, the possibility of a collision was uppermost in Commodore Brook's mind. His fears were realized when, shortly before midnight, the rear ship of Column 10, the small Dutch timber carrier *Berkel*, tangled with the 3,177-ton Danish steamer *Bornholm* in the adjacent Column 9. The master of the *Berkel* later reported that he had been forced to go to port by the 5,528-ton *Commandant Dorise*, which had strayed from Column 11. In doing so, *Berkel* found herself heading straight for the *Bornholm*. The *Berkel* went hard to starboard and full speed astern, but it was too late. She slammed straight into the Danish ship, holing her in her engine room. On the following day the *Bornholm* was taking on so much water that she was in danger of foundering. Commodore Brook ordered her to make a dash for Reykjavik, some 430 miles to the north. With the help of a salvage tug which came out from Iceland she reached Reykjavik on the night of the 27th, by which time she was in a sinking condition. ONS 5 had lost its second ship.

The *Bornholm's* assailant, the *Berkel*, was able to continue her voyage with nothing more than a bent stem, in spite of the steadily deteriorating weather. Convoy speed over the twenty-four hours from noon on the 25th to noon on the 26th was no more than 2–3 knots, with many of the ships in ballast virtually hove-to through-out the 26th. The *Penhale*, a 19-year-old British steamer of 4,000 tons, fell so far astern that it was considered unwise for her carry on. Commodore Brook ordered her to join the *Bornholm* in Reykjavik.

The convoy was now down to forty-one ships, but the deficit was more than made up later on the 26th, when B-7's second destroyer HMS *Vidette* joined from Iceland, bringing with her three additional ships. The British steamer *Bosworth* and the Norwegian *Gudvor* were dropouts from a previous convoy ONS 3, while the American fleet tanker *Sapelo* had delivered a cargo of oil to Reykjavik and was on her way home.

By this time Commander Gretton had become extremely concerned at the state of *Duncan*'s bunker tanks, which were again at a low ebb. The weather was still so bad that any attempt at topping up from the tanker *British Lady* would have been foolhardy. In desperation, Gretton contacted the Admiralty in Liverpool requesting permission to leave the convoy and make a quick dash for Greenland, the nearest possible bunkering station. This was not an option he chose lightly, for at this time of the year Greenland was in the ice pack, no place for a thin-hulled destroyer to venture. Fortunately, over the following twenty-four hours the weather showed a rapid improvement, and both *Duncan* and *Vidette* were able to refill their tanks from the *British Lady*.

The sun shone while the two escorts were bunkering, and there seemed to be no end to ONS 5's good fortune, as air cover arrived unexpectedly in the form of two Lockheed Hudsons from Iceland, and at the same time Commander Gretton received word that the eastbound convoy HX 234, then passing to the south of ONS 5, was being attacked by a U-boat pack. Bad news for the eastbound convoy, of course, but a very welcome diversion for Gretton's ships, which were now running into poor visibility. There seemed a very good chance that ONS 5 might slip past the U-boats while they were busy with HX 234.

HX 234, a convoy of thirty-nine loaded ships, escorted by the destroyers HMS *Highlander* and *Vimy* and the corvettes *Pennywort* and *Rosthern*, had sailed from New York on 12 April. The Convoy Commodore Captain E. C. Denison RN wrote in his report:

> The first intimation that the convoy was being shadowed was at 04:00/21 when HMS *Pennywort*, stationed on the

starboard quarter of convoy, attacked a U-boat in position 56° 27'N 47°30'W. Course and speed of the convoy at the time was 074° 9½ knots. It was known that Convoy ONS 3 was being attacked to the southeast and that Convoy ON 178, steering south 150 miles ahead of HX 234, had been sighted and reported. Course of the convoy was immediately altered to 050° and 040° at 12:00/21. Course was again altered to 047° after dark at 21:30/21.

A strong Northerly gale had meanwhile sprung up with heavy snow blizzards and during the night the speed of the convoy was reduced to 3–4 knots . . . Very heavy snow storms were encountered during the night of 22/23 which were of great assistance in hiding the convoy, which was not attacked . . . At 02:00/23 HMS *Vimy*, who was on the starboard beam of the convoy, reported two submarines on the surface bearing 210° 15 miles, and attacked with depth charges . . . The Senior Officer Escort estimated that 12 U-boats were concentrated on convoy April 23rd . . .

Despite the appalling weather conditions and the strength of the enemy, HX 234 lost only two ships, the 10,218-ton ex-Danish passenger ship *Amerika*, sailing under the British flag, and the 7,176-ton American Liberty *Robert Gray*; another British ship, the *Silvermaple*, was damaged. However, this sacrifice was not entirely in vain, as it undoubtedly distracted attention from ONS 5 as it passed to the north.

The sudden deterioration in the weather also came as a bonus to ONS 5, but the convoy's luck was about to run out. At noon on the 28th HMS *Duncan*'s wireless operators picked up transmissions from a U-boat which appeared to be directly ahead of the convoy and very close. The visibility at the time was only 3 miles, but the destroyer gave chase at full speed. Nothing tangible was seen, and Gretton concluded that the unidentified U-boat had either sighted the convoy or detected the ships with her hydrophones. He knew that it was only a matter of time before reinforcements were called in and a concerted attack on his convoy began.

ONS 5's lone tracker was U-628, a Type VIIC under the command of Oberleutnant Heinrich Hasenschar. She had sailed from Brest on 8 April and after a difficult crossing of the Bay of Biscay, harassed by patrolling Allied aircraft, she had joined four other boats in an attack on Convoy HX 233. The eastbound convoy of fifty-eight ships, having left New York on 6 April, was then less than 500 miles south-west of the Fastnet.

Heinrich Hasenschar's War Diary reads:

> 0743   Have contact on convoy.
> The attack begins immediately because little time remains before dawn. I manage to push through the screen unnoticed between the forward flank destroyers cutting sharply across to within approximately 5,000 metres of the convoy. The convoy is arrayed in 2 or 3 columns in line ahead in a long formation. At least 25 very big, heavily laden ships are present, however there are probably more. Between the ships, or at a short lateral distance, two other escorts can be seen.

> 0745   I had intended to shoot at two overlapping freighters each 2 double shots. The first, a fan from tubes I and III, was fired by hand without targeting due to a crewman's error.

> 0747   Fan from tube II and IV on two medium-sized freighters lying deep in the water. Target speed 8 knots, target angle 75, estimated range 4,000 metres, depth 7 metres.

> 0749   Turned for a stern shot from Tube V on the following freighter . . . After 3 minutes 55 seconds a hit on the forward freighter, two seconds later a pistol detonation is clearly heard in the boat. Apparently a Pi-failure. After approx 3 minutes (time not clocked) running time approx 4½ minutes hit on most recently fired at freighter, forward of bridge. Bright flash, otherwise no direct effect noted. The first ship hit sets a white masthead light.

Hasenschar's hit was on the 7,134-ton British-flag steamer *Fort Rampart*. Built in Vancouver and owned by the US War Shipping Administration, she was a wartime replacement lend-leased on bareboat charter to the Ministry of War Transport, who had put her under the management of Charlton, McCallum of Newcastle. Deep-loaded with 8,700 tons of general, and a full timber deck cargo, she was making her maiden crossing of the Atlantic. Hasenschar claimed a second hit on the US tanker *Harrison Smith*, but she was unharmed.

HX 233's escorts were quick to act, racing in to saturate the area with depth charges. But they were not quick enough; Hasenschar had gone deep, and was already out of Asdic range.

Although badly holed, the *Fort Rampart*, buoyed up by her timber deck cargo, was still afloat when, four hours later, Hasenschar came across her, abandoned and drifting astern of the convoy. He administered what he thought was the coup de grâce with another torpedo, but still the *Fort Rampart* refused to sink. She was finally sent on her last voyage by Rolf Borchers in U-226 in the early hours of 18 April.

Having decided to leave the *Fort Rampart* to her fate, Hasenschar continued on his way to the west, reaching U-628's allotted patrol area, 750 miles due east of St John's, at noon on 22 April, coincidentally just as the first ships of Convoy ONS 5 were arriving in the North Channel 1,500 miles to the east. Three days later, U-628 became part of *Gruppe Specht*. This group of seventeen boats was positioned in a 250-mile-long chain running in a south-easterly direction from a point 340 miles due south of Cape Farewell. With the boats 13–14 miles apart, that is within surfaced visibility of each other, *Specht* effectively formed an impenetrable fence across ONS 5's projected course.

For the next eight days the *Specht* boats patrolled up and down at an economical speed of 6 knots, always with an empty horizon. It was monotonous work and would have been insufferably dull had it not been for the challenging North Atlantic weather. With the wind blowing force 6 from the north-west, the sea rough, and fierce squalls of rain and sleet, life in the conning tower was uncomfortable, cold and wet, but never boring.

Encouraged by the successful pack attack on the eastbound convoys SC 122 and HX 229, Admiral Dönitz was determined to keep up the pressure on the Allies. Contacting every U-boat operational in that part of the Atlantic, he eventually gathered together a force of fifty-eight boats. Over the following forty-eight hours he then set up three patrol lines straddling the convoy lanes. *Gruppe Specht* with seventeen boats was already in position and was joined by *Gruppe Meise* with thirty boats and *Gruppe Amsel* with eleven. Drawn up in north-south patrol lines to the east of Greenland, the three packs formed an impenetrable barrier covering all the approaches to and from the USA and Canada. They represented the largest submarine combat force ever concentrated in the Atlantic in all the six years of the war, a wall of torpedoes and guns through which no Allied ship could pass unchallenged. And yet, as if to emphasize the vastness of the great ocean, three convoys in succession, ONS 4, westbound with forty-two ships, ON 179, fifty-four ships also westbound, and the eastbound HX 235 of forty ships, all somehow managed to slip through the net unseen. Only ONS 5, which was unfortunate enough to be approaching the patrol lines when the code-breakers at Bletchley Park had been temporarily left floundering by the addition of a fourth rotor to the German Navy's Enigma, was caught in Admiral Dönitz's spider's web.

On the morning of 28 April ONS 5 was some 400 miles to the east of Greenland's Cape Farewell and making a good 8 knots on a south-westerly course. To everyone's great relief, the Atlantic had ceased to rage and roar, the unceasing gales having given way to a light southerly breeze, slight sea and low swell. But it was not all sweetness and light. The convoy's northerly routing had brought it to within a few degrees of the Arctic Circle, and the cold was intense and bone-penetrating. The streaming oilskins of the past days had been replaced by duffel coats and heavy woollens, and there was a sheen of ice on the decks. For those manning the bridges of the ships, the lookouts and guns' crews, watch-keeping was as much a test of endurance as ever.

Noon came, and the hopeful navigators stood by with their sextants, but the sky remained stubbornly overcast, and there were no sun sights. Position-fixing, as it had been for much of the passage so far, was by dead reckoning, or 'by guess and by God' as the more phlegmatic would have it. Estimated positions were exchanged between ships by lamp, and thoughts were turning to lunch, when HF/DF operators in the escorts obtained a fix on W/T transmissions close ahead of the convoy.

Commander Gretton, assuming the transmissions were from a U-boat, took *Duncan* ahead at full speed, hoping to catch the enemy on the surface, but the visibility had fallen to less than

3 miles, and nothing could be seen. An Asdic search was carried out, but the U-boat had obviously dived and made its escape.

The U-boat *Duncan* had failed to flush out was U-650, another Type VIIC on her maiden war patrol. She had sailed from Bergen only ten days earlier, with 27-year-old Oberleutnant Ernst von Witzendorff in command. An officer who had spent most of his service in motor torpedo boats, Witzendorff was on his first voyage in command of a U-boat. Detecting the approach of the destroyer, he had taken advantage of the falling visibility to make good his escape, and despite being forced to dive on three occasions by patrolling Allied aircraft, had maintained contact with the convoy. He reported his sighting to Lorient, who ordered him to shadow the convoy until reinforcements arrived.

An entry in Dönitz's War Diary for the day reads:

> As the weather was variable during the day, visibility sometimes as much as 2,000 metres, no boats with the exception of U 650 were able to approach the convoy. The boats' messages were also very inaccurate and they had overestimated the convoy's speed. The boat was requested to send D/F signals about 2–3 hours before darkness. Two other boats then came up shortly before dusk on the D/F signal, U 386 and 378. Both reported the enemy's position: U 378 at 0232 in AD 7941 and U 386 at 0155 in AD 7864. As these positions are so far apart from one another, the boats were requested to examine the grid given. However, no other messages have been received since 0300 on the morning of the 29th.

A careless flurry of W/T traffic between the gathering U-boats alerted Commander Gretton to the danger, and in company with the frigate *Tay*, *Duncan* carried out a series of depth charge attacks on Asdic contacts. All showed no result. The chase continued into the night, with the U-boats probing ONS 5's defences from all sides, but always being beaten back by a wall of depth charges. From the number of HF/DF contacts being reported it was obvious that the convoy was now surrounded by U-boats. In fact, seizing the opportunity to score another major victory, Dönitz had hastily formed a new pack, codenamed *Star*, consisting of fifteen boats, with the specific aim of dealing with ONS 5. The new group comprised U-192, U-209, U-231, U-258, U-378, U-381, U-386, U-413, U-528, U-532, U-533, U-552, U-648, U-650 and U-954.

Aware of the danger the convoy faced, Gretton reported the situation to Liverpool, where the Submarine Tracking Room immediately ordered the 3rd Support Group, consisting of the destroyers HMS *Impulsive, Offa, Panther* and *Penn*, to sail from St John's and render assistance.

Midnight came and went with the unending crump of exploding charges welcoming in the new day, and still no blow was landed by either side. Then, at 0132 on the 29th, HMS *Snowflake* obtained a firm hydrophone contact and homed in on it, sighting a U-boat on the surface at a range of 1,300yds. She was U-532, a new Type IXC long-range boat under the command of Korvettenkapitän Ottoheinrich Junker, a 38-year-old with many years service in submarines.

Junker was quick to aim the first blow, firing a volley of six torpedoes at the approaching corvette before crash-diving. The blow failed to land, all six torpedoes missing *Snowflake*, one by a mere 20yds. The corvette retaliated, lunging after the fast disappearing U-boat and following her down with three depth charges set to shallow. Asdic contact was made soon afterwards at 200yds, and the corvette followed with a 10-charge pattern. By this time, HMS *Tay* had joined the hunt, and between them the two escorts smothered the area with depth charges.

That the U-boats were not having it all their own way is illustrated by an extract from Dönitz's War Diary:

> The weather conditions showed no improvement on the 29th. The wind SSW 6, seaway 4, snow squalls and poor visibility were reported. Owing to W/T interference boats were unable to communicate with the Command on the night of 28/29th and it was not until midday on 30th that messages were again received from the boats. According to these, the last convoy contact message originated at 1150 in AK 1236 on course of 240 degrees. U-650 attempted to attack the convoy in this position, but was picked up by a destroyer using radar before the attack. Contact with the convoy was not re-established. U-386 reported difficulty

in submerging after depth charge attack and withdrew for repairs.

Dawn came early on the 29th, the first streaks of pale grey showing on the eastern horizon shortly before 0400. U-258, with Kapitänleutnant Wilhelm von Massenhausen in command, which had been hogging the shadows on the fringe of the convoy throughout the night, now moved ahead at full speed, submerging when she was directly in the path of the convoy. And there she waited with all tubes loaded, von Massenhausen listening for the approach of the ships with his hydrophones.

On the bridge of HMS *Duncan*, Commander Peter Gretton, his face grey and lined from lack of sleep, was keeping a dawn vigil. Reports flooding in indicated that at least five or six U-boats were stalking the convoy, and Gretton feared that it was now, at the hour when all human life was at its lowest ebb, that they would strike. He had distributed his escorts to form a defensive screen around the convoy, but with only two destroyers, a frigate, four corvettes and a trawler to protect thirty-eight helpless merchantmen, it was a pitifully thin screen. Gretton later put his thoughts down on paper:

> The convoy, still unscathed, was in good order and the weather was now better. After seeing that all the escorts were in their day stations I went below for a sleep. About five minutes after leaving the bridge the alarm bell rang and I dashed back. 'Ship torpedoed astern', the OOW reported, and we could see that one ship had hauled out of line to avoid her next ahead. The group at once carried out the routine search plan for the U-boat. Extremely difficult to determine from which side the torpedo had been fired. That the sight of the explosion in the water was well outside the convoy was a great help, for another of the same salvo of torpedoes had exploded at the end of its run after passing through several columns without hitting another ship. The submarine must have fired from between the columns very close to her target.

While Gretton was on his way down to his sea cabin below the bridge, the leading ships of the convoy had passed over the submerged U-258. Von Massenhausen had then brought her up to periscope depth between columns 3 and 4. It was now full daylight, or as light as it was likely to get, the sky still being a low overcast. The wind continued to blow strong from the south-west, the sea rough, the swell big and menacing. Visibility hovered from poor to near zero as blinding snow squalls swept in from time to time. Some of the merchant ships, particularly those in ballast, were having great difficulty in staying on station. Among them was the US-flag steamer *McKeesport*.

The 6,198-ton *McKeesport*, built in 1919 for US Lines Inc. of New York, was feeling the weight of her years, even though she carried only 2,000 tons of sand ballast. Commandeered by the US Government in 1939, she had almost from the outset of the war been engaged on a continuous shuttle, carrying Red Cross supplies for the many thousands of refugees in Europe fleeing before the advance of Hitler's Panzers. In 1940 she was credited with 'literally preventing starvation for an estimated 1 million men, women and children in refugee camps'.

Captain Oscar J. Lohr, commanding the *McKeesport*, was only too well aware of how vulnerable his ship was on this grey morning in April 1943 as she sailed in the ranks of ONS 5. She was No. 42 in the convoy, second ship of Column 4, and as such she was relatively well protected, but her ancient steam turbine was fighting a losing battle with the Atlantic weather, and she was gradually dropping astern.

The *McKeesport* was the proverbial lame duck, and as such ripe for harvesting. Her potential executioner had her in his sights and was awaiting the opportunity to act. This came at 0729, by which time the *McKeesport* was straggling in the wake of the convoy. Von Massenhausen fired a spread of three torpedoes, one of which hit the *McKeesport* on her starboard side in way of the forward end of her No.1 hold. The effect was spectacular, the force of the explosion sending a column of dirty water laden with shredded tarpaulins, broken hatch boards and sand ballast high in the air. The sea poured through the jagged hole torn in the side of the ship, and she began to list heavily to port.

The reaction of ONS 5's escorts had been instantaneous. *Northern Gem* and *Snowflake*, being the nearest at hand, both made Asdic contact and raced in to drop depth charges. These appeared to have no obvious effect, but it was later learned that U-258 had received considerable damage and was forced to return to her Biscay base.

Although he feared that his ship was mortally hit, Captain Lohr decided to continue steaming at full speed, hoping to maintain contact with the convoy, but after about 45 minutes he was forced to admit defeat. The list had increased to 20°, and the ship was so far by the head that it was becoming impossible to hold her on course.

Reluctantly, Lohr rang the engines to stop and, when the way was off the ship, gave the order to abandon. With some difficulty, due to the heavy list and the weather prevailing, the *McKeesport's* four lifeboats were launched, and all sixty-eight crew abandoned ship. They were picked up within 30 minutes by the trawler *Northern Gem* and later landed in St John's. There was only one casualty, Able Seaman John Anderson who died of exposure after being rescued. He was buried at sea.

Contrary to expectations, the *McKeesport* stayed afloat for many hours after she was abandoned by her crew. When Commander Gretton discovered that confidential books and charts had been left on board, he sent HMS *Tay* back with orders either to recover these or sink the torpedoed ship by gunfire. However, although the frigate made an extensive search she failed to find the wreck. In fact, the American ship had already been found by U-258 and sunk with two torpedoes.

When word reached the Admiralty of the attack on ONS 5, it foresaw a dangerous situation arising and immediately called on reinforcements for Gretton's escorts. The destroyer *Oribi* was detached from the eastbound convoy SC 127, while four other destroyers, HMS *Impulsive, Offa, Panther* and *Penn* of the 3rd Support Group, sailed from St John's with orders to join the threatened convoy as soon as possible. Unfortunately, coincident with their sailing there was a rapid deterioration in the weather, and by the late afternoon of the 29th a full gale was blowing in the area. At 1700 HMS *Sunflower* reported that she had been struck by a rogue wave that had swamped her crow's nest, and *Oribi* was reduced to 11 knots. It was almost midnight before she reached ONS 5, being the first of the support ships to arrive.

While ONS 5 had only just begun her struggle against the storm-force winds and mountainous seas of the notorious Western Ocean, some 850 miles to the west U-203 a new addition to *Gruppe Specht* had reached her allotted patrol area south of Cape Farewell.

U-203, commissioned in Kiel in February 1941 by Kapitänleutnant Rolf Mutzelburg, was a Type VIIC ocean-going boat with a record of being dogged by bad luck. Her troubles had begun in the summer of 1941, just a few weeks into her first war patrol, when she was heavily depth charged by two British destroyers in the North Atlantic. She escaped, but had been significantly, though not critically, damaged. Two months later, while she was attacking Convoy HX 73, the British frigate *Larkspur* had laid about her with twenty-six depth charges, but again U-203 had escaped without any serious harm. Another month passed, and she was caught on the surface by a patrolling British aircraft which bracketed her with a stick of depth bombs. Once more she got away, this time with superficial damage to her casings.

Further into the winter of 1941, while crossing the Bay of Biscay, U-203 was again caught unawares on the surface by a British aircraft, and the U-boat was so badly damaged by depth charges that she was forced to return to port for repairs. She was back at sea a month later, when Rolf Mutzelburg lost his life in a tragic accident.

U-203 was hove-to on the surface in fine, calm weather in a deserted spot off the Azores, and Mutzelburg had allowed his men on deck to breathe the clean air and take a dip in the comparatively warm sea. While they were frolicking in the ocean, Mutzelburg was tempted to join them. He stripped off and dived from the conning tower, but as he did so, the boat rolled in the swell, and Mutzelburg struck his head on the casing. He died from his injuries the next day.

U-203 returned to Brest, where Kapitänleutnant Hermann Kottmann was appointed to command. Whereas Rolf Mutzelburg, who ran a tight but happy ship, was well liked by his men, not surprisingly they took an immediate dislike to Kottmann. He was ex-Waffen SS, a committed Nazi and thoroughly unpleasant in his dealings with his crew.

An American Intelligence Officer who later interrogated Kottmann described him as being one of the most unpleasant U-boat captains he had encountered, adding, 'He was arrogant, overbearing and demanding. It was impossible to conduct a civil conversation with him ... He is a fanatic Nazi and is best described as a military robot. Any cultural or humanitarian impulse which may exist in his make-up has been completely sublimated by political and military indoctrination to which he has been subjected.'

Embarking on her eleventh war patrol, with Hermann Kottmann still in command, U-203 sailed from Brest on the afternoon of 3 April 1943 in the midst of an air raid on the port. Because of the intense activity by Allied aircraft, her passage across the Bay of Biscay was fraught with danger. Travelling submerged by day and on the surface at night, her progress was frustratingly slow. She had finally reached her patrol area on the 22nd, and was promptly depth charged by a British destroyer. Twenty-four hours later, she had sighted a British corvette, and Kottmann lost no time in trying to torpedo her. Both his torpedoes missed, and U-203 suffered the inevitable depth charging.

Easter Sunday, the 24th, dawned fine and clear, and with it came the escort carrier HMS *Biter*, on her way to cover the two westbound convoys ONS 4 and ON 179. U-203 was still on the surface, and in the half-light Kottmann failed to notice that *Biter* had one of her aircraft in the air, and that her escorting destroyer HMS *Pathfinder* was nearby. The result of Hermann Kottmann's negligence was a complete disaster for U-203. Both aircraft and destroyer raced in to attack, forcing the U-boat to dive so quickly that her diesel exhaust valve was left open as she went down. Her engine compartment flooded, and Kottmann was unable to go deep to avoid the shower of depth charges that followed the boat down.

Pathfinder dropped forty depth charges in all, smashing most of U-203's instruments, and as the water in her hull rose, the boat began to sink stern-first. All available crew members were sent forward to try to adjust the trim, but the downward slide continued. Before it was too late, Kottmann gave the order to blow tanks, and U-203 shot to the surface. Hatches were thrown open, and her crew tumbled out on deck. *Pathfinder* moved in and picked up Kottmann and thirty-nine of his crew. Ten others lost their lives, trapped in the U-boat as she spiralled to the bottom of a very dark and cold ocean.

Now that the attack on ONS 5 was gathering pace, Dönitz was calling in all boats within striking distance. Among those who answered his call was U-227, then just six days into her first war patrol and passing north of the Faroe Islands.

Commanded by 25-year-old Kapitänleutnant Jürgen Kuntze, newly promoted and in his first command after only five months service in the U-boat arm, U-227 had an unfortunate start to her career. Commissioned in Kiel in the late summer of 1942, while working up in Danzig Bay she had struck a British mine and was so badly damaged that she was fortunate to be able to make port. Luckily, none of her crew were seriously injured, but the repairs needed to the boat would keep her out of service for almost nine months.

When she was finally ready for active service, U-227 was ordered to break out into the Atlantic and head west to join the others who were engaged in harassing Allied convoys off Newfoundland. Anxious to take part in what was said to be another turkey shoot, Kuntze opted to remain on the surface day and night while passing through the dangerous waters between the Faroes and Iceland. This proved to be a very bad decision.

Air cover for the North Atlantic convoys had been increasing for some time, bolstered by the stationing of 455 Squadron RAAF at Benbecula in the Outer Hebrides. The primary role of 455 Squadron, which flew Handley Page Hampden torpedo bombers, was to patrol the waters of the Northern Transit Zone, through which the U-boats passed on their way out into the Atlantic.

U-203 had sailed from Kiel on 24 April, and was passing through the Northern Transit Zone late on the 30th. The weather was typical for that latitude, with rain squalls sweeping across the face of a turbulent sea, reducing visibility and giving, in the opinion of Jürgen Kuntze, sufficient cover for U-203 to remain safely on the surface. However, his lookouts failed to see Hampden X/455, piloted by Sergeant J. S. Freeth, as she came in low from astern. Freeth's depth charges caught U-203 just as she was about to crash-dive, blasting open her pressure hull. She rolled over and plummeted to the bottom, taking Kuntze and his crew of forty-eight down with her.

Unheard and unseen by the men of ONS 5, the number of U-boats lined up against them had already been reduced by two.

CHAPTER NINE

Storm Force

By daybreak on the 30th, ONS 5 was in 60° north, some 300 miles east of Cape Farewell. The weather had deteriorated further, the wind increasing to Storm Force 10, bringing with it, to quote the Beaufort Scale:

> Very high waves with long overhanging crests. The result-
> ing foam in great patches is blown in dense white streaks
> along the direction of the wind. On the whole the surface
> of the sea takes a white appearance. Tumbling of the sea
> becomes heavy and shock-like. Visibility affected.

This was the North Atlantic aroused. And to complete this scene of utter misery, the convoy being so far north, the surface of the sea was littered with drift ice and small icebergs. The wind being in the south-west, almost right ahead, the ships were slamming into the oncoming seas with sickening force. For the box-shaped merchantmen every wave was a brick wall, and station-keeping was becoming a near impossibility. The slimmer, smaller escorts were suffering even worse, bouncing from wave-top to wave-top, periodically disappearing in a welter of spray and spume.

Inevitably, the merchant ships began to scatter again. Five were forced to give up the fight and drop out of the ranks altogether. The Norwegian-flag *Gudvor* was first to go, followed by three British ships, *Director*, *Dunsley* and *Omega*, then the 43-year-old Greek-flag *Nicolas*. All were in ballast and pitching so heavily they were barely making any forward progress. By noon the five stragglers were out of sight 30 miles astern and, much against his better judgement, Commander Gretton was forced to detach the corvette *Pink* to look after them. In effect, the five became a sepa-rate convoy, with Lieutenant Robert Atkinson, commanding HMS *Pink*, in absolute charge.

During the night, the gap left by *Pink* was filled by the arrival of the 34-knot fleet destroyer *Oribi*, a veteran of both the Malta and the Russian Arctic convoys. She had been ordered out from

Iceland by Western Approaches Command in Liverpool. With the help of *Oribi* and a Coastal Command Liberator from Ireland, which appeared overhead at 0645, Gretton was able to keep the U-boats at bay. *Oribi*, after her high-speed dash, was already dangerously low on fuel, but fortunately, during the course of the morning there was a slight improvement in the weather, and she was able to top up her tanks from the *British Lady*.

The lull in the weather was short-lived, for as the sun climbed behind the clouds, so the barometer began to fall again. By late evening it was blowing a full gale once more, and the merchantmen were labouring in the heavy swell, their decks awash with spray and spume. The escorting destroyers, built for speed rather than stability, were again taking the worst punishment, rolling and pitching like demented stallions. Only the tub-like corvettes, purpose-built for the foul North Atlantic weather, were riding more or less comfortably. But as the night progressed, so the destroyers made deep inroads into their fuel reserves, and unless the weather soon eased sufficiently for them to refuel, some of them would need to leave before long for St John's.

The situation was worsening by the hour. Now the visibility was falling, hiding the probing U-boats from Gretton's ships, whose radars were rendered almost useless by the clutter on their screens generated by the breaking waves. The escorts were doing their utmost to protect their charges by dropping small patterns of depth charges at random, but this in itself was probably more of a danger to the escorts than to the enemy. In the appalling weather prevailing, even the destroyers, for all the horsepower they had below, were unable to make more than 8 or 9 knots without incurring damage to themselves. Depth charges dropped at that speed were liable to blow their sterns off. The only escort to make any useful contact was the corvette *Snowflake*, which picked up a surfaced U-boat on her radar at 3,000yds. She immediately ran down the line of bearing firing star shell, opening up with her 4-inch and Oerlikons when the submarine came in sight. The startled U-boat was forced to dive in a hurry. *Snowflake* followed her down with a pattern of depth charges, but contact was lost.

ONS 5 survived the night intact, and the first day of May dawned with the weather being described by Gretton as 'alarming'. The wind was back up to force 10, gusting to 11, more or less halting all forward progress. An extract from the log of Commodore

Brook reads: 'Half convoy not under command, hove to and very scattered'. This chaotic situation prevailed throughout the day and the following night, the convoy logging just 20 miles for the twenty-four hours. However, what affected the convoy also applied to the U-boats, who were too busy fighting their own personal battles with the wind and waves to contemplate an attack. A number of ships were already straggling astern, including the twin-screw Blue Funnel cargo liner *Dolius*. Her steering gear had broken down under the strain of the weather, and she was reduced to steering with her engines just to hold her bow-on to the seas. The *Dolius* was a well-found Clyde-built ship fitted with hydraulic steering gear, and for that to break down was an indication of just how severe the weather was. Due to the superhuman efforts of her engineers, the *Dolius* was under way again by nightfall and making all speed to rejoin the convoy. In view of later events, it might have been better if she had not bothered to rejoin.

The storm did not ease until the morning of the 2nd; only then could Brook and Gretton begin sorting out the sorry mess Convoy ONS 5 had become. This was done with the help of a lone Liberator which had flown over 1,000 miles from Iceland to give brief air cover to the convoy. Several hours later, the remaining thirty-two ships were in some semblance of order, and convoy speed had increased to 5 knots. But there were other problems to come, indicated by the presence of small growlers and isolated floes. They were nearing the main ice pack.

The fortunes of ONS 5 improved somewhat when, after dark, ships of the 3rd Support Group finally arrived from St John's. The 'rescuing cavalry' comprised the destroyers *Offa, Panther, Penn* and *Impulsive*, all under the command of Captain J. A. McCoy RN in HMS *Offa*. Being senior in rank to Commander Gretton, McCoy could have displaced him as Senior Officer Escort, but he chose not to do so, thus avoiding an awkward situation.

With no fewer than seven destroyers, a frigate, three corvettes and two armed trawlers now screening them, the ships of ONS 5 were so well protected that the pack of U-boats surrounding them were unable to move in close enough to mount an attack. The weather, although considerably improved, remained a problem, but the night of 2/3 May passed relatively quietly. Now, however, the question of refuelling once more reared its frustrating head. The weather was still too rough for the fleet oilers to do their work, and HMS *Duncan* was critically low on fuel, so low, in fact, that unless she refuelled within the next few hours, Gretton might be left with a dead ship on his hands. As it was, he had just enough oil on board to reach St John's – if he left at once. It was time for a decision to be made.

The weather prevented Gretton from transferring his command to another ship, and in the end he was forced to bow to the inevitable. On the afternoon of the 3rd he used the radio telephone to hand over command of the escort to Lieutenant Commander Robert Sherwood in the frigate HMS *Tay*. A seasoned North Atlantic convoy man, Sherwood was ideally suited to take charge of the group. An ex-Merchant Navy officer, he had first gone to sea in 1922, joining the Royal Naval Reserve in 1929. Thereafter he had served as a sub-lieutenant in minesweepers, and then in one of HM's battleships. On the outbreak of war in 1939 he was appointed to command the ASW trawler HMS *Spurs*, and in 1940 assumed command of the corvette HMS *Bluebell*. In 1942 he was given command of HMS *Tay*.

Having briefed Sherwood, Gretton set course for St John's steaming at 8 knots, at which speed he calculated *Duncan* would be able to reach port without her tanks running dry. He later wrote:

> It was a bitter blow to have to leave the convoy on May 3rd when it was still in the danger area. No other course of action was possible. The weather throughout was extremely bad and consistently adverse. I took every precaution to fuel at every available opportunity and was indeed fortunate to get a short lull in the gales to top up *Duncan*, *Oribi* and *Vidette*. The convoy took 16 days to get from Oversay to Westomp.

HMS *Duncan* arrived in St John's with just sixteen tons of fuel remaining in her bunker tanks.

The night of 3/4 May was a repeat of the previous night, with the convoy's escorts fighting a desperate running battle to keep the probing U-boats at bay. They succeeded in doing so, but it was a long, punishing night for all involved. When a grey dawn struggled to disperse the gloom on the morning of the 4th, Lieutenant Commander Sherwood found himself facing the first major crisis of his new command.

With the coming of the new day the weather had moderated slightly, the wind dropping to force 6, no more than a strong breeze, but the sea was as rough and angry as ever. After the exertions of two nights past, three of the newly joined destroyers of the Support Group, *Impulsive*, *Panther* and *Penn*, reported to Sherwood that they were in dire need of fuel. All three made repeated attempts to top up from the *British Lady*, but each time the rough seas prevented the bunker hose from being coupled up. In the end, Sherwood had no other option but to authorize the detachment of all three to replenish their tanks, *Impulsive* to Iceland, *Panther* and *Penn* to St John's. At the same time, he ordered the trawler *Northern Gem*, which had on board sixty-seven survivors from the *McKeesport*, to make for St John's before her food and water gave out.

The defence of ONS 5 was now in the hands of three destroyers, a frigate, three corvettes and an armed trawler. Two of these destroyers, *Offa* and *Oribi*, would be in need of fuel within the next twenty-four hours. The state of the convoy was moving towards critical again, and when Sherwood signalled Liverpool to this effect, the 1st Support Group, consisting of the frigates *Jed*, *Spey* and *Wear*, and the sloops *Pelican* and *Sennen*, was ordered to sail from St John's and make all speed to join ONS 5. The group left St John's at midday on 4 May.

ONS 5 was now some 500 miles to the north-east of St John's and steaming at 7 knots in comparatively good order. The weather was continuing to improve, the wind having eased to no more than a fresh breeze. White horses were still running, although they were more playful than threatening, and the long Atlantic swell rolled in less ponderously. If these conditions persisted, another seventy-two hours would see the ships off Newfoundland and within reach of ample protection by air and sea. Lieutenant Commander Sherwood had good cause to think that the worst was over.

The U-boats were still there, of course, hovering on the outskirts of the convoy, and Lieutenant Commander Sherwood was obliged to make the best possible use of his limited resources to keep them at bay. The sister destroyers *Offa* and *Oribi* were stationed well in the van, radars and Asdics sweeping ahead to flush out any U-boats in the convoy's path; further back, *Vidette* was guarding the starboard bow, while *Sunflower* kept watch on the port bow.

The main body of the convoy was covered by *Snowflake* on the port beam and *Loosestrife* to starboard. Bringing up the rear was the trawler *Northern Spray* on the starboard quarter, while HMS *Tay* was hovering on the port quarter, from where Sherwood was able to keep a watchful eye on proceedings. In retrospect, it was a pitifully inadequate defence against the number of U-boats believed to be in the vicinity of ONS 5, but it was the best that could be done.

For Dönitz's U-boats, the anticipated rout of ONS 5 was not going according to plan. To date, they had sunk just two stragglers, both carrying nothing more significant than sand ballast, and this at the cost of two of their number and ninety-five irreplaceable submariners. Anxiously awaiting news of an anticipated victory in his eyrie overlooking the river at Kerneval, Karl Dönitz was far from pleased when word arrived of the German casualties. He was even less pleased when he received the news that, at the same time as U-209 was under attack, another Canadian Catalina operating out of Gander had surprised Heinrich Heinsohn's U-438 on the surface 200 miles south of Greenland and crippled her. This was not the way it was supposed to happen, and Dönitz began to question the dedication of his U-boats. This prompted him to send the following signal to his Atlantic packs:

> You are better placed than ever before . . . Don't overestimate your enemy, but strike him dead.

Throughout the day the bad news continued to flood in. Shortly before dark that afternoon, HMS *Vidette* found U-630 motoring on the surface and smothered her with depth charges as she crash-dived. Under the command of 25-year-old Oberleutnant Werner Winkler, U-630 was on her first war patrol, which had begun in Kiel on 18 March and to date had gone well, Winkler having sunk two ships in Convoy HX 231 on 5 April, albeit vessels already abandoned after being torpedoed by other U-boats. After her brush with *Vidette*, U-630 was not heard of again, and was assumed to have been sunk with all hands.

There was little rest for *Vidette* that evening. Lieutenant Commander Raymond Hart explains:

> For *Vidette* that night's battle started at 2200 (2000 Convoy Time) when a radar contact was obtained at 3,600 yards.

We closed at best speed and when, within a few hundred yards the U-boat dived, we gave him a pattern of 14 depth charges and then returned to our station on the convoy. Half an hour later another radar contact was obtained and we gave chase again and when, within a few hundred yards and in the excitement of the moment, I gave the order to stand by to ram. I almost immediately regretted it as the U-boat began diving so I tried to avoid running over the top of him and delivered him instead 14 depth charges. If I had succeeded in ramming, I probably would have severely damaged *Vidette* and been useless as an effective escort and become a liability to the convoy instead. I made a positive decision there and then, not to ram if the opportunity was offered again. This U-boat may have been U-270 which *Vidette* was credited with damaging.

As darkness closed in that evening, the convoy ran into patches of fog, dense at times. The thirty-one remaining ships, covered by McCoy's two destroyers, Sherwood's frigate, HMS *Vidette* and the corvettes *Loosestrife*, *Snowflake* and *Sunflower*, huddled closer together, anxious to maintain contact in the falling visibility. HMS *Pink* and her auxiliary convoy, namely the Norwegian-flag *Gudvor*, the three British ships *Director*, *Dunsley* and *Omega*, and the Greek tramp *Nicolas*, were somewhere lost in the gathering gloom astern, while six more stragglers rounded up by the trawler *Northern Spray* were making all speed to catch up. A seventh, the ex-French steamer *Lorient*, could not be found, having dropped back over the horizon out of sight.

The 4,737-ton *Lorient*, built on the Tyne in 1921 for Compagnie Delmas-Vieljeux of Paris for the West African trade, had been seized by the Royal Navy off the Canary Islands in February 1941 and handed over to the management of Evan Thomas Radcliffe of Cardiff. Now flying the Red Ensign and manned by a full British crew led by Captain Walter Manley, the *Lorient* was bound for Halifax in ballast.

It is not known exactly what happened to the *Lorient*, except that on 6 May the US Coastguard cutter *Manhassett* reported sighting an abandoned merchantman some 350 miles due south of Cape Farewell. Nearby were some empty lifeboats and fragments of wreckage. There was no sign of life aboard the ship, and no bodies were seen in the water. The *Manhassetts* lost sight of the derelict during the night, and next morning she had disappeared, presumably sunk. What happened to the *Lorient's* crew of forty-six must forever remain a matter for conjecture, for no trace was ever found of them.

One of the six stragglers rounded up by the *Northern Spray* was the 4,635-ton *North Britain*, then 6 miles behind the rear ships of ONS 5.

Commanded by 38-year-old Captain John Bright, the *North Britain* was owned by the North Shipping Company of Newcastle, a 'one-ship outfit' with its roots back in the days of sail. The *North Britain* was of very basic design, a wartime replacement built in South Shields in 1940 to fill one of the many gaps left by Dönitz's torpedoes. She carried a total complement of forty-six, including eight DEMS gunners, her accommodation being arranged in typical 1930s style, with officers and catering staff amidships under the bridge, ratings and petty officers aft beneath the poop, sailors to starboard and firemen to port. The naval gunners also lived aft, below decks in quarters erected in the 'tween deck of her after hold.

Being on light draught, with only 993 tons of firebricks and fire clay to give her stability, the *North Britain's* single propeller, half out of the water, was working overtime as she struggled to rejoin the convoy. She was steering a straight course, not zig-zagging, making her the perfect target for a well-aimed torpedo; and Oberleutnant Günter Gretschel was well placed to take advantage.

Gretschel was in the conning tower of U-707, a Type VIIC he had commissioned in Hamburg in July 1942. She was on her second war patrol, having sailed from St Nazaire on 17 April. In ten months of active service she had sunk only one ship, the 7,176-ton American Liberty *Jonathan Sturges*, bound across the Atlantic with 1,500 tons of sand ballast.

The *Jonathan Sturges*, only six months out of the Delta Shipyard in New Orleans, had already carried one cargo to Britain and was homeward bound with Convoy ON 166, which consisted of forty-nine merchantmen, escorted by seven ships of the American Escort Group A-3.

ON 166 sailed from Liverpool on 21 February 1943, at a time when both Allied and German intelligence services were reading each other's encrypted messages with comparative ease. Consequently, the *Jonathan Sturges* found herself embroiled in a deadly game of cat and mouse in mid-ocean.

Having listened in to U-boat radio traffic in the North Atlantic, the Admiralty had routed ON 166 further to the south than normal, hoping to avoid detection. Meanwhile, Berlin had received word of the convoy's sailing and had assembled a wolf pack of nineteen U-boats to waylay it.

ON 166 was in mid-Atlantic before Dönitz's pack caught up with it, and from then on boat after boat broke through the escort screen to loose off its torpedoes. In this grim fight to the death, which raged for six days and six nights, fourteen Allied merchant ships were lost, in return for three U-boats sunk and three so damaged that they had to return to base.

Günter Gretschel's U-707 was one of the last of the pack to make contact, when she homed in on two stragglers from the convoy, the Dutch steamer *Madoera* and the *Jonathan Sturges*. Under the cover of a passing rain squall, Gretschel fired two torpedoes, both of which hit the American Liberty, breaking her back. Fifteen men were killed by the torpedoes, while the rest got away in three lifeboats and four rafts. One of the lifeboats capsized in the heavy seas, but its occupants were picked up by the other boats. The subsequent fortunes of the survivors serve to illustrate some of the chaos reigning in the North Atlantic at that time.

Three days after the *Jonathan Sturges* sank, one of her lifeboats with twenty-three men on board came across a lifeboat from the *Madoera*, which had been sunk by another U-boat minutes after the American. The Dutch lifeboat carried only three Lascar seamen, so to even up the numbers, six men transferred to it from the American boat. The *Madoera's* boat then picked up twelve men from the *Jonathan Sturges'* liferafts, and this boat spent another thirteen days at sea, before being rescued by the US destroyer *Belknap*. The American lifeboat, with seventeen survivors on board, subsequently disappeared without trace. The same fate befell another of the *Jonathan Sturges'* boats, also carrying seventeen.

Although the *North Britain* was easy prey, Gretschel chose to ignore her, intending to get ahead of ONS 5 and submerge, allow the lead ships to pass over him, then resurface in the heart of the convoy, where he would be in position to wreak havoc.

Under the cover of darkness, U-707 overtook ONS 5 with ease, but Gretschel had not reckoned on the two destroyers *Offa* and *Oribi* being stationed ahead of the convoy. When U-707 submerged, she was immediately detected by *Oribi's* Asdic, the destroyer being hidden in the darkness only 1,000yds from the U-boat.

Oribi dropped a pattern of eight depth charges close to U-707, forcing her to go deep to avoid damage. For a while Gretschel listened to the thunderous beat of the propellers as the convoy passed overhead, and he was about to come back to the surface when U-707 was caught in *Tay's* Asdic beam. More depth charges came spiralling down to explode all around the U-boat, sending shock waves through her hull and forcing her to stay down. By the time she was free to surface, the convoy was several miles ahead and heading towards the horizon at a fast pace. Gretschel was left with the target he had first sighted, the *North Britain*.

On the bridge of the *North Britain* all attention was focused on the dark shadows on the horizon ahead, which was all that could be seen of the disappearing convoy. No one had eyes for the long, sinister shape of U-707 approaching on the port beam. Unseen, the U-boat closed the range to 1,500yds, at which Günter Gretschel fired a fan of three torpedoes from his bow tubes.

At that range Gretschel could not possibly miss, and at least two of his torpedoes went home in the British ship's after hold, breaking her back. The time she took to go down was estimated variously between sixty-nine seconds and four minutes, but all accounts said her end was very quick. Captain Bright, realizing that his ship was doomed, immediately ordered his crew to abandon her. He then went below to his cabin to collect the ship's papers. This instinctive action was to cost him his life, for he was never seen again.

The *North Britain* slid under stern-first, so fast that most of those in the crews' accommodation right aft were trapped and went down with her. It is probable that these men, sailors, firemen, gunners, were asleep, for this was after midnight. The rest of the crew, those who had been in the midships accommodation or on watch on the bridge, made strenuous efforts to launch the lifeboats, but only one boat succeeded in leaving the sinking ship's side, and that was waterlogged.

In all, only fifteen men successfully abandoned ship, and of those four died of exposure before they were picked up by the trawler *Northern Spray*. Lieutenant F. A. J. Downer, commanding HMS *Northern Spray*, later wrote in his report:

> At 0024Z 0n 5 May 1943, while moving from position 5 in DE 8 to position H in NE 6, the S.S. *North Britain*, a straggler, was torpedoed. The ship had a defective boiler and the defect had just been made good and speed increased to rejoin the convoy when the torpedo struck aft, the ship went down stern first in about two minutes. Observation was carried out around the spot without gaining contact. At first it was thought there were no survivors as no boat or lights could be seen, and a signal was sent to HMS *Tay* to that effect.
>
> At 0055Z, however, some lights were seen and at 0105Z we commenced picking up survivors from a raft and a waterlogged lifeboat. The lifeboat was brought alongside time and time again but the occupants did not make much effort to get out and the line parted after about five or ten minutes. Eventually at 0230Z 10 survivors from the boat and one from the raft were on board. There was still one light in the water and course was altered towards it and the ship was just steadied up when it disappeared and no sign of any of the survivors could be seen.

It was some small consolation that while this grim drama was being enacted, HMS *Vidette* was hitting back at the enemy. She had detected Hans-Jurgen Auffermann's U-514 on her radar at 3,600yds and had given chase with all guns blazing. U-514, a Type IXC, was on her third war patrol, having already enjoyed considerable success in attacking other convoys. Since first joining the fray in August 1942, she had sunk a total of 38,000 tons of Allied shipping, an achievement which earned Auffermann the Iron Cross 1st Class. Now he was eager to add to that total. Moreover, he was still smarting from his treatment at the hands of British air patrols while crossing the Bay of Biscay outward bound. Reluctant to submerge in daylight and prolong the crossing of the danger zone, he had twice been caught on the surface and strafed and bombed. Miraculously, U-514 escaped serious damage, and only Auffermann's confidence had been dented.

U-514 was again on the surface, but it was a dark night, and she was trimmed right down so that only her conning tower was above water. It was this that showed up on *Vidette*'s radar. Auffermann cleared the bridge and crash-dived when the destroyer was seen bearing down on them at speed, but he was not quick enough. *Vidette*'s depth charges followed the U-boat down, damaging her periscope and starting a serious leak in her stern tube. The damage put her out of the battle for forty-eight hours.

Half an hour later, *Vidette*'s radar picked up another surfaced U-boat at 3,600yds. The destroyer raced in to attack, and at 1,000yds another small echo came up on the screen. U-662 and U-732 were lying in wait for ONS 5 and had apparently failed to notice *Vidette*'s approach.

U-662, under the command of Heinz-Eberhard Müller, was also on her third war patrol, having sailed from Lorient on 23 March. Six days later, she was ordered to join in a pack attack on the northbound convoy SL 126. There was immediate success for Müller when he fired a spread of four torpedoes into the convoy, sinking two ships and damaging another. Another thirty-seven empty days were to pass, and U-662 was due to return to Lorient, when ONS 5 came her way. Anxious to make one more kill before setting course for home, Müller had been careless in his approach. He was fortunate in that U-662 escaped with nothing more than a severe shaking up from *Vidette*'s depth charges.

The Danzig-built U-732, commanded by the inexperienced 24-year-old Oberleutnant Claus-Peter Carlsen, had left Brest on her maiden voyage on 8 April with orders to join a 'large patrol line' which was then forming up south of Greenland. On the outward passage Carlsen claimed to have sunk 'a munitions ship escorted by four destroyers and a corvette'. He stated that, at the time, the visibility was very poor, and his torpedo was fired with the aid of radar. Thereafter, this mystery ship became known as the 'Radar Steamer', as she was reputed to be the first ship ever detected and sunk by radar.

Carlsen also claimed to have sunk a 6,000-ton freighter in ONS 5, but again this kill appears to have been a figment of his fertile imagination. In fact, in U-732's one and only attack on ONS 5, she was lucky to survive. Carlsen failed to see *Vidette* until she was within 80yds of his boat, and suffered accordingly. As U-732 made a belated crash-dive, the destroyer attacked with depth charges, causing sufficient damage to require Carlsen to run for Biscay for repairs. *Vidette* had lived up to her reputation by putting two of Dönitz's grey wolves out of the battle, thereby shortening the odds against the survival of ONS 5.

CHAPTER TEN

Black May

Called from his bunk by the strident clamour of alarm bells, Bill Skinner reached the bridge of the *Harbury* to find it a haven of calm. Despite the noise and pyrotechnics set up by HMS *Vidette*'s rout of the U-boats, Captain Walter Cook and the officer of the watch were in the darkened wheelhouse conversing in quiet tones as they followed the action through their binoculars. In each wing of the bridge duffel-coated DEMS gunners, strapped into the harness of their 20mm Oerlikons, methodically quartered the dark night with their long-barrelled guns. There was no evidence of panic; the scene was almost unreal. But then there was little else the crew of this lumbering merchantman could do, other than wait for events to unroll.

Like the majority of British merchantmen, the *Harbury* had not been built with war in mind, but she was heavily armed. She mounted a 4-inch anti-submarine gun aft, a 12-pounder on the poop deck above it, two Oerlikons on the bridge and two on the boat deck, along with two twin .303 Marlins and various rockets to deter low-flying aircraft. At first glance, this would seem to be a formidable array of weaponry for a merchant ship, but in reality offered little more than a show of force. Her main adversary, the German U-boat, attacked unseen, the crash of her torpedo against the ship's side usually being the first, and only, indication that the enemy had arrived. By then, not all the guns in the world would help her.

During the course of that day at least fifteen U-boats were known to be in contact with ONS 5. Among them was U-628, which had been patiently shadowing the convoy since early morning, reporting back to Lorient at regular intervals.

U-628, a Type VIIC commanded by 27-year-old Heinrich Hasenschar, had left her berth in Brest on 8 April on her third war patrol. Having successfully run the gauntlet of Allied aircraft in the Bay of Biscay, she was 650 miles out into the Atlantic when she was directed to join in a wolf-pack attack on HX

233, a 54-ship convoy bound from New York to Liverpool. The convoy was well defended by a combined British, Canadian and American escort force, which duly repulsed the attack, Hasenschar having to be content with picking off the 7,134-ton *Fort Rampart* while she was straggling astern. Loaded with 8,700 tons of timber and steel, the British ship was on her maiden voyage, having sailed from Vancouver, where she was built, some six weeks earlier. For the *Fort Rampart* it was a sad end to a long and rather pointless maiden voyage. For Heinrich Hasenschar and U-628 it was a small triumph, not to be repeated until the Atlantic was crossed.

Seventeen days later, on 4 May, when he was ordered to join in the attack on ONS 5, Hasenschar made the following entry in his War Diary:

5.3.43

00.50   WSW 4, Sea 3-4, abating. Vis. good, light swell.

With the beginning of twilight, about 01.30 hours, I begin to draw slowly closer in order to attack if possible right at the beginning of the night. During twilight the starboard forward sweeper positions far to the west, while the second destroyer pushes ahead to the south. I succeed in breaking through the gap between them, and in the meantime in the partial darkness gain contact and immediately begin the attack. By my observation the convoy is formed in a double V-formation (Rhombus).

Because the forward escort has pressed a little bit to the north, the across distance will be quite large, so that I arrive at the shooting position at an already blunt angle to the forwardmost ships. To manoeuvre ahead by running along appears not advisable because in the meantime the flank escort is moving closer, so I am forced to shoot from a greater range. Because the firing solution is based on precise plotting I decide on aimed single shots in spite of the long range.

The nearest ship in the starboard column shows at the point of firing a target angle of 90°, the most forward 120°–130°. The 2nd and 3rd ships are the big ones, the rest medium freighters.

02.43–02.46 Single shots from tubes I-IV on different freighters from the forward to the after ones. Targeting constantly updated. Distance 4–5,000 metres, target speed 8 knots, depth 3 metres.

Remaining on the surface, Hasenschar fired a total of six torpedoes, including one from his stern tube. He later claimed one large freighter sunk, another probably sunk and a third set on fire. His attack complete, he then dived and ran clear of the convoy, before stopping and returning to periscope depth. With only one torpedo remaining in his tubes, he retired to reload, intending to return later in search of another target. The entry in his War Diary reads:

With the approach to the shooting location numerous illuminated lifeboats are sighted. A short time later, a shadow with a weak red masthead light. Shows at first little target angle, moved off a little. Ran along briefly and then closed with diesel at KF. While closing a corvette is recognized which now lies stopped. Bow right, target angle 110°. Closed to about 800 metres.

0502 Shot from tube III.

After 28 seconds an enormous tongue of flame, a shower of sparks, then nothing more. A strong pressure wave follows. I suppose that the whole depth charge load has exploded. The corvette is literally atomised. Directly after the shot a second shadow is sighted approximately 2,000 metres to starboard, also with red masthead light. Turned away and ran off to the north at AK. Shadow becomes gradually weaker and is lost from sight. Since I have fired all but the damaged upper deck torpedoes, and as of now 8 boats have contact with the convoy, I decide to remain by day in the sinking area to search for disabled vessels.

The corvette must have been a figment of Heinrich Hasenschar's overwrought imagination, for no escort vessel was reported lost or damaged that night. In fact, all the torpedoes U-628 fired appeared to have missed, except the one that hit the *Harbury*.

The muffled thud of the torpedo exploding and the shock of the ship recoiling from the massive explosion that blew her hull wide open were not new to Third Officer Bill Skinner. Acting instinctively, he went to the wing of the bridge intending to fire the white distress rockets, signalling to the rest of the convoy that the *Harbury* had been torpedoed, but they were already soaring up into the night sky.

Captain Walter Cook described the events that followed in his report to the Admiralty:

> No-one saw the track of the torpedo, which struck my ship on the starboard side in No.5 hold. There was a loud explosion, no flash was seen, but a large column of water was thrown up. The hatches were blown off No.5 hold, which flooded immediately. The after peak bulk-head collapsed and the tunnel door fractured, through which the engine room flooded slowly. I made my way to the bridge, and observed that the vessel was settling rapidly by the stern. The 2nd Officer fired the rockets, and I switched on the red light. The Confidential Books were thrown over the side, and a distress W/T message transmitted. The Chief Engineer stopped the engines, and reported to me that in his opinion the shaft had been bent by the explosion.

To add to the horror of the night, the *Harbury*'s main generator was knocked off its base by the explosion, and the ship was plunged into complete darkness. Within minutes she was list-ing heavily to starboard and so far down by the stern that her after well deck was under water. An inspection of the damage by torchlight showed that the ship was beyond saving. Without hesitation, Captain Cook gave the order to abandon.

Although most of the *Harbury*'s crew had been asleep when she was hit, no one had been reported injured, and there was no outbreak of panic, as might have been expected under the circumstances. Captain Cook later remarked on this, saying, 'All my crew behaved exceptionally well throughout, and no one showed the least sign of panic.'

It was only when it came to swinging the boats out that things started to go wrong. It was then discovered that the starboard quarter boat had been thrown out of its davits by the blast of the exploding torpedo, and the port lifeboat had also been dislodged and fouled its bowsing-in wires. Moreover, there was still a heavy swell running, and when this was combined with the complete darkness, the operation of lowering the boats deteriorated into a shambles.

The port quarter boat capsized on hitting the water and was lost, leaving some men marooned in the after part of the ship. As the seas were already breaking over the after deck, these men were forced to jump overboard, and some of them were lost. Finally, with order restored, the two large lifeboats on the boat deck were successfully launched, and the majority of the *Harbury*'s crew got away.

True to the tradition of the sea, Captain Cook stayed with his ship, opting to take one last look around to make sure no one was left behind. Two other crew members, Able Seaman Robertson and Able Seaman Gunner Maclean, volunteered to stay with him. The Second Officer was instructed to hold his boat alongside to take all three off when the search was finished. This boat was secured alongside with a rope painter, but such was the violent rise and fall of the swell that the rope parted, and the boat and its occupants vanished into the night.

Meanwhile, Captain Cook and the two seamen had made a thorough search of the ship for other survivors. Cook wrote in his report:

> Robertson, Maclean and I then searched all the 'midship accommodation to see if anyone was left aboard; we could not get aft, as the well deck was flooded, so we shouted as loudly as we could, but received no answer. I assumed that everyone had left the ship. Towards midnight, we heard a grinding and wrenching noise from aft, and thinking that the vessel was about to sink the three of us went forward and boarded the forward starboard raft. We cast off the painter, as the raft was bumping heavily against the ship's side, and drifted away from the vessel. We lay to the sea anchor, and could see two white lights in the distance, which I assumed belonged to the 1st and 2nd Officers' lifeboats. At 0120 on 5th May we saw a shower of sparks, followed by a violent explosion, which appeared to be on the surface of the sea, approximately one or two cables from the raft. A dense cloud of black smoke drifted across the water.

Cook and his two companions were saved from the misery of a long night adrift when, at about 0230 on the 5th, their raft was sighted by the armed trawler HMS *Northern Spray*, which had been designated as rescue ship for ONS 5. The trawler already had a number of survivors on board from other sunk ships, and during the course of the next hour or so she came across the *Harbury*'s lifeboats. When Captain Cook called the roll, he found that of the *Harbury*'s total complement of forty-nine, all but seven were safe on board the *Northern Spray*. The missing men were assumed to have been lost in the heavy seas when they jumped from the sinking ship's after deck.

At daybreak it was found that the *Harbury*, although low in the water, was still afloat, and Captain Cook agreed with Lieutenant Downer to try to re-board her. Cook later wrote in his report:

> The First Lieutenant from the trawler, my Chief Officer and I re-boarded the ship at 0630 on the 5th May. We found there were six to eight feet of water in the engine room and stokehold, the after well deck was under water, with the poop deck just awash, the stern being so low that the sea was pouring into No.4 main hold from the 'tween decks. We stayed on board half an hour collecting stores, and left the ship at approximately 0730. I did not see my ship again, but in view of her condition I am certain she eventually sank. Aircraft were sent out the following day to the scene, but no sign of the ship could be found.

The *Harbury* was, in fact, still very much afloat, but her luck ran out when she was found again by Heinrich Hasenschar in U-628.

After emptying his tubes into ONS 5, Hasenschar had made off to the north-east, but had not left the area. U-628's stock of torpedoes now being exhausted, she was awaiting word from Lorient to rendezvous with a supply U-boat to restock and, at the same time, top up her fuel tanks and take on fresh stores. Then Hasenschar proposed to return to the attack on the convoy.

At 0908, while U-628 was still loitering at periscope depth awaiting orders, Hasenschar caught sight of a merchant ship on fire and apparently abandoned. A small escort vessel, probably a corvette, was standing by her. Assuming the derelict to be one of the ships he had torpedoed during the night, Hasenschar decided to wait for the escort to leave and then finish her off with his deck gun.

It turned out to be a long wait, being past noon before the escort steamed out of sight over the horizon. Then, surfacing just enough to bring U-628's conning tower clear of the water, Hasenschar approached the wreck cautiously. When he was within about 500yds he stopped and examined the blackened ship through his binoculars. There appeared to be no sign of life on board, and as the lifeboat davits were empty, it seemed safe to assume she had been abandoned. Bringing the U-boat's casings above water, Hasenschar sent his 88mm gun's crew forward with orders to deliver the coup de grâce.

Although she was heavily by the stern, with her after holds almost certainly flooded, the *Harbury* – for it was she – being a typical product of the River Clyde shipyards, did not surrender to the deep easily. Hasenschar's gunners used up their entire remaining stock of forty rounds of 88mm, and a further 100 rounds of 20mm armour-piercing shells, before the British ship could be induced to sink below the waves. Then a rather disgruntled Heinrich Hasenschar left to keep his rendezvous with the supply boat.

While Hasenschar was engaged in sending the *Harbury* to her last resting place 2,000 fathoms down in the cold Atlantic, some 10 miles astern of the collection of stragglers following in the wake of ONS 5, U-209 was closing in.

U-209, under the command of 40-year-old Rhinelander Heinrich Brodda, was entering the Battle of the Atlantic for the first time. From her first day of active service, in March 1942, she had been engaged in hunting Allied shipping in the cold grey waters of the Barents Sea, a mission in which she had failed miserably. In twelve months in Arctic waters she had succeeded in sinking only 1,356 tons of shipping, specifically two Soviet tugs and their tows. When it was later learned that the barges under tow by the two tugs were carrying Russian political prisoners consigned to forced labour, and that more than 300 had perished in the sinkings, Brodda felt he had achieved nothing to be proud of. Other than twice coming under fire from ships of the Royal Navy, and each time escaping undamaged, U-209's record in those waters was best forgotten.

Heinrich Brodda was a rare breed of U-boat commander, having come up through the ranks of the German navy. He was believed to have entered the service as an enlisted seaman in the mid-1920s, emerging as Leutnant zur See in minesweepers in 1940. He was undoubtedly a seaman of considerable experience, but the extent of his expertise in U-boats is uncertain.

Sailing from Kiel on 6 April 1943, U-209's introduction to the Atlantic battle was quick and uncompromising. Passing to the south of Iceland and heading west on the surface, she was pounced upon by a B-17 'Flying Fortress' of No. 220 Squadron RAF which showered her with depth bombs. Fortunately, Brodda was quick to dive, and U-209 once more escaped, but this time with a damaged periscope.

On the afternoon of 4 May, while she was homing in on ONS 5, U-209 was again caught on the surface, this time by a Catalina of No. 5 Squadron RCAF on convoy protection duty from Gander. The Catalina swooped on the U-boat, dropping a stick of depth charges that exploded close enough to cause extensive damage, including knocking out her main radio transmitter. U-209 escaped, but not scot free. She was apparently unable to dive safely, and without her radio could not inform BdU of her predicament. U-209 was last heard of on 6 May, when she passed a message to Lorient through U-954. Lorient ordered Brodda to return to base for repairs, but the boat failed to reach port. Exactly what happened to her may never be known, but it is assumed that she must have been lost in a diving accident as the result of damage inflicted by the Canadian aircraft's depth charges.

At noon on 4 May ONS 5 was 450 miles to the north-east of St John's and making all speed for the safe waters that lay to the south. However, realizing that the remaining ships of the convoy were now in imminent danger of being completely wiped out by the horde of U-boats surrounding them, C-in-C Western Approaches ordered Escort Group 1, Support Group to go to their rescue. The Support Group, based in St John's, consisted of the Egret-class sloop HMS *Pelican*, commanded by Commander Godfrey Brewer RN (S.O), the ex-US Coastguard cutter, now a Banff-class sloop, HMS *Sennen*, and the River-class frigates *Jed*, *Spey* and *Wear*.

Sennen had engine problems and was unable to sail, so at noon on the 4th Brewer took the other ships of the group to sea, leaving the sloop to follow as soon as she was able. The weather on sailing was fine and clear, and the four ships set off to the north at 16 knots, expecting to meet up with ONS 5 at about 0700 next morning. Unfortunately, Commander Brewer had not reckoned with the notorious Grand Banks fog, which duly came down during the course of the afternoon of the 4th, reducing the visibility to 400yds. In the interest of safety, the four ships slowed to a walking pace, and the ETA at the convoy became a matter for speculation.

When the Support Group left St John's, U-438 was some 200 miles south of Cape Farewell and making full speed on the surface to join in the assault on ONS 5. In command of the boat was Korvettenkapitän Heinrich Heinsohn, who had replaced Rudolf Franzius at short notice. This was U-438's fourth war patrol and Heinsohn's first patrol in the senior rank, having been promoted whilst at sea.

Heinsohn had already felt the effect of increased Allied air cover; at first light that morning the boat had been surprised on the surface by a Catalina of No. 5 Squadron RAF. Fortunately for Heinsohn, his lookouts were wide awake when the flying boat put in an appearance, skimming the wave-tops. The conning tower was cleared in record time, and U-438 dived just fast enough to avoid the full force of the aircraft's depth bombs, escaping with minor damage to her casings. She was less fortunate, however, when that night, back on the surface, she showed up on HMS *Pelican's* radar. Commander Brewer reported:

> Wake was observed when the range was about 500 yards, close under the starboard bow. At 0407 (0107 convoy time) the S/M was sighted fine on the starboard bow at 300 yards range steering 180°. When the U-boat was just starting to dive fire was opened by A and B guns. Up to this time she must have been unaware of Pelican's presence, as from the relative speed of approach she was only doing 9 knots and was fully surfaced when sighted.
>
> When about 100 yards or less from the ship and fine on the port bow, the U-boat crash-dived, turning to port as she did so. The ship was just starting to swing to port under full rudder and the bows swung just inside the conning tower swirl. A 10-charge pattern set to 50' and 150' was fired, the first charge being let go into the swirl. There were no failures and all 10 charges fired. Contact

was regained astern but the echo was very weak and hard to follow.

Between half a minute and a minute after all depth charges had exploded, the Officer in Charge and most of the D/C crew reported seeing two thin founts of water, resembling shell splashes, astern close to where the pattern had exploded.

When the range was about 800 yards course was altered to bring contact ahead and it was again attacked at 0415. During this attack the target was moving very slowly right with slight closing inclination and contact was again held down to practically zero range. Nine charges set to 150' and 300' were fired and all charges exploded. Nine charges only were fired as the cartridge case of the port after thrower had been blown from the breech into the expansion chamber during the first attack and was not cleared in time to allow that particular thrower to be ready for the second attack.

During the whole of this second attack very slow HE was heard and various odd noises which sometimes resembled an E/S set being switched on for short periods.

After firing the second pattern no contact could be regained, although own wake and D/C disturbance were both picked up 1½ minutes after D/Cs had exploded 3 small sharp explosions were heard together with other miscellaneous noises, mostly resembling, as before, an E/S set being switched on for short periods. About nine minutes later, i.e. 10½ minutes after second pattern was fired, two further explosions were heard, the second one being violent enough to shake the ship. All five explosions were very sharp and resembled torpedoes or D/Cs exploding.

No wreckage was seen and contact could not be regained after sweeping through the area and it was decided therefore to carry out operation 'Observant' as it was considered from the accuracy of the first attack that if the S/M was not definitely destroyed then at least she would not be able to dive and therefore might attempt to escape on the surface especially as the visibility was down to less than half a mile. This produced no results and as the close screen of ONS 5 had by this time been reduced to two effective ships, the hunt was abandoned, it being my considered opinion that the U-boat was either destroyed or so severely damaged that she could no longer be a menace to the approaching convoy.

'Black May', as May 1943 became known in German naval circles, had begun for Dönitz's U-boats, and it would spread across the length and breadth of the Atlantic. To quote an unnamed German naval commentator:

After our successful battles in March, we had to return many U-boats back to ports for repairs and improvements. There may be code decryption by the British, and I seriously suspect so. On the 24th our great U-710 had been sunk by the air escort for the convoy. We are continuing to get hit hard and it seems like the enemy is making progress in anticipating and attacking our Wolf Pack. There may be a reversal in battle plans as our night strategy is being imitated by the Allies. Thus we shall surface and strike in the day, but I doubt truly that this will produce any considerable results. Surface escorts only are defeating our U-boats! There is a serious fog problem as well, but this seems to be an issue that is commonplace in the areas of hot and cold gulf stream conflate. We are going to lose a few U-boats here, for the first time in the war.

Admiral Dönitz, now Commander-in-Chief of the Kriegsmarine, added his thoughts:

The ONS-5 onslaught has been the downfall for us. We are getting into real trouble now, and I am concerned at the amount of U-boats being sunk. We fight on, but there seem to be some serious problems ahead of us.

And there was worse to come.

On 25 April, U-659, under the command of Korvettenkapitän Hans Stock, had sailed from Brest with orders to join eight other boats in setting up an east-west patrol line some 500 miles west of Cape Finisterre. The object of the group was to ambush a southbound British convoy said to consist of twenty-eight landing craft, escorted by two armed trawlers and a minesweeper.

Two days later, on the 27th, U-439, commanded by Oberleutnant Helmut von Tippelskirsch, left Brest charged with the same mission. The two U-boats were destined to meet, with disastrous consequences for both.

U-659 arrived in the patrol area on 1 May. The weather there at the time was wretched, with gale-force winds, a rough sea and fierce rain squalls bringing zero visibility at times. There followed forty-eight hours of miserable up-and-down patrolling, battered by wind and sea, with U-659's conning tower mostly awash and, as the visibility was so poor, with the added danger of running into the next boat in the line.

By this time U-439 had also arrived on the scene, and at about 2300 on the 3rd she was the first to sight the southbound convoy. Von Tippelskirsch reported the sighting to Lorient and was ordered to shadow the British ships, at the same time acting as a beacon for the other U-boats to home in on. During the night, von Tippelskirsch was given permission to attack. He overtook the convoy and then manoeuvred into position to attack from ahead.

Unknown to von Tippelskirch, Korvettenkapitän Stock in U-659 had decided to adopt the same method of attack. The two boats were, in fact, then steering parallel courses in very close proximity and hidden from each other by the blinding rain. At about 0215 on the 4th von Tippelskirsch made a slight alteration to port, which immediately put the two U-boats on converging courses. Minutes later, U-439 was brought up short with a shuddering crash.

Hans Stock was in the conning tower of U-659 with his first watch officer, a seaman petty officer and two lookouts, but none of them saw the razor-sharp bows of U-439 rearing up out of the darkness on the starboard beam. There was a loud crash, a grinding of metal upon metal, and U-659 heeled hard over to port. Water poured into her control room through a jagged gash in her side, quickly followed by a gush of diesel oil from a punctured fuel tank.

Realizing that his boat was sinking under him, Stock ordered his crew to don lifejackets and abandon ship. The order came too late for most of U-659's crew, who were trapped below. A few reached the deck and jumped over the side, but as they did so, a large wave hit the stricken U-boat, and she rolled over. U-659 sank in less than five minutes after the collision, taking Hans Stock and forty-three of his men with her.

Aboard U-439, similar chaos reigned. When U-659 had loomed up out of the darkness, von Tippelskirsch had gone full astern on both engines, but it was too late. U-439's bows were ripped open in the collision that followed, leaving her torpedo tubes open to the sea, while the effect of going full astern in heavy weather had flooded her exhausts and filled the boat with diesel fumes. It soon became evident that she, too, was sinking, and von Tippelskirsch gave the order to take to the water.

Waves were breaking over U-439 as she slewed beam-on to the sea, and she was quickly swamped. She went down with a rush, most of her crew again being trapped in her hull. From the two lost U-boats, only twelve men were saved by the convoy's escort vessels.

On that same day, some 600 miles south-west of Ireland, the U-boats suffered another blow when a Liberator of 86 Squadron RAF, flying out from Aldergrove to provide cover for the east-bound convoy HX 236, picked up a radar echo on the sea. This proved to be a U-boat on the surface, the long-range Type IXB U-109, then embarking on her ninth war patrol. In command was 27-year-old Oberleutnant Joachim Schramm.

U-109, a Type IXB, was one of Dönitz's U-cruisers, displacing 1,051 tons on the surface and with a range of 12,000 miles. Powered by two MAN M9V 40/46 supercharged 4-stroke, 9-cylinder diesels, which gave her a top surface speed of 18¼ knots, she was armed with six torpedo tubes and twenty-two torpedoes, along with the usual 105mm deck gun, all of which made her a force to be reckoned with. However, since first venturing out into the Atlantic in May 1941, her record had not been impressive. In three years and eight lengthy patrols, reaching as far as the Gulf of Guinea and the east coast of South America, she had sunk just twelve Allied merchantmen. From four of those patrols she had returned completely empty-handed, having failed to fire a single torpedo or shell with intent.

When U-109 was spotted by the RAF Liberator in mid-Atlantic, her ninth patrol, and her career, came to a sudden end. The U-boat's lookouts were caught napping, and the big, four-engined bomber swooped before she had time to dive. An accurately dropped stick of depth bombs straddled U-109 as she blew tanks, inflicting heavy damage. She disappeared beneath the waves, surfacing again some minutes later. She then began to sink, and although there was ample time for her crew to escape, her hatches remained firmly shut. U-109 went to the bottom taking Oberleutnant Joachim Schramm and his crew of fifty-one with her.

CHAPTER ELEVEN

A Good Night's Work

Kapitänleutnant Hartwig Looks and the US freighter *West Maximus* were contemporaries, both born in the shadow of the Great War of 1914–1918, but on opposite sides of the Atlantic Ocean. Looks first saw the light of day in Flensburg, Germany, and the *West Maximus* in the yard of Skinner & Eddy in Seattle, USA. They were destined to meet in conflict some twenty-five years later.

Originally built for the US Navy as an auxiliary, the *West Maximus* was a Type 1013 cargo vessel, better known as a 'Hog Islander'. She was of 5,561 tons gross and powered by a steam turbine driving a single screw which gave her a service speed of 11 to 12 knots. The Great War ended before she was completed, and she was handed over to the US Shipping Board, who put her into service carrying relief cargoes from America to war-ravaged Europe. In 1923, along with hundreds of other wartime-built ships, she became surplus to requirements and was laid up in a backwater of the Gulf of Mexico.

In mid-1940, after seventeen years swinging to an anchor, her hull encrusted with weed and barnacles, the *West Maximus* suddenly found herself wanted again. For the second time in twenty-one years Europe was at war, and American shipping was at a premium. She was taken out of mothballs, reconditioned and put back into service under the management of Moore-McCormack of Baltimore. When America went to war again in December 1941, she joined the North Atlantic shuttle carrying vital war materials between the US and Britain. On 3 April 1943, then under the command of Captain Earl E. Brooks and at the end of another of her endless transatlantic voyages, she arrived in Liverpool to discharge. Three weeks later, she joined Convoy ONS 5 for the return passage to New York, carrying just 745 tons of sand ballast.

The career of Hartwig Looks had progressed along familiar lines; joining the Kriegsmarine as an officer cadet in 1936, when war broke out three years later he was serving with the 2nd Destroyer Flotilla. In April 1940 he came ashore to join the staff of the Admiral Norwegian North Coast, but in December of that year, anxious to play a more active part in the war, he volunteered for the U-boats. After suitable training, he served as First Watch Officer under Jürgen Koenkamp in U-375 in the Mediterranean until March 1942, when he was given command of the Type VIIC U-264, then under construction at the Bremer Vulkan yard at Vegesack. With the rank of Oberleutnant zur See, Looks commissioned U-264 in May 1942 and moved into the Baltic for trials and exercises.

U-264 started life under a cloud. Things began to go wrong as soon as she left her fitting out berth in Kiel. Shifting her berth, she rammed the quay wall and damaged her bows. Fortunately, the damage was only superficial and quickly repaired, but it seems that a pattern had been set, for whilst engaged on torpedo trials in the Bay of Danzig, she inadvertently torpedoed another U-boat. Accidents do happen when live ammunition is being used, but in this case the U-boat on the receiving end happened to have on board a party of top-ranking officials from the German Ministry of Propaganda who were observing the trials. Their boat was badly damaged and only just managed to stay afloat until she could be beached. Some time later, while on tactical exercises in the same area, the unfortunate U-264 rammed another boat, U-444, which was also exercising. In this case the damage was slight, but Oberleutnant Looks must nevertheless have heaved a huge sigh of relief when, on 10 January 1943, he sailed from St Nazaire for faraway West African waters.

The first war patrol of U-264 proved to be unfruitful and completely unfulfilling for Hartwig Looks and his crew. Her only warlike action during the seven weeks she combed those sub-tropical waters came when she fired a spread of torpedoes at some Allied ships anchored off Casablanca, all of which missed. She was ordered to return to St Nazaire in mid-February, and on her way north was detailed, along with two other U-boats, to act as escort for the blockade-runner *Hohenfriedburg*. This German tanker was carrying a much-needed cargo of oil from the Far East to Bordeaux. The accident-prone U-264, having somewhere along the way damaged one of her propellers, was running on one engine, and as her top speed on the surface was 10 knots, she was assigned as close escort to the *Hohenfriedburg*. The other U-boats were stationed 20 miles on either side of the tanker.

When this unusual convoy was passing to the west of Lisbon, a warship was sighted which turned out to be the British heavy cruiser HMS *Sussex*. The escorting U-boats immediately dived, and U-264, approaching to within 5,500yds of the cruiser, fired a spread of four torpedoes at her. All four missed their target, and HMS *Sussex* retaliated by opening fire on the *Hohenfriedburg* and sinking her. Once again, Hartwig Looks had missed the opportunity to make a name for himself and his boat. He did, however, redeem himself by picking up all eighty-five men of the *Hohenfriedburg*'s crew, whom he landed in Lorient. There U-264's propeller was repaired, and she then returned to her base at St Nazaire.

U-264, with Hartwig Looks newly promoted to Kapitänleutnant still in command, sailed from St Nazaire on 8 April 1943, bound for the waters off Cape Farewell. On her way west she was ordered to join other boats in an attack on the eastbound convoy HX 233, then passing 400 miles north of the Azores. Approaching the convoy on 17 April, U-264 was detected by the escorts and subjected to such a fierce and prolonged depth charging that she was forced to withdraw. She had suffered severe damage, but her crew were able to carry out running repairs, and she was soon on her way to the west again.

When U-264 reported to Lorient that she was ready for action again she was ordered to join in the attack on Convoy ONS 5 then in progress. She arrived within sight of the convoy just before midnight on 4 May.

It was a black, moonless night, with a rough sea and heavy swell running, but the visibility was very good. Hidden in the darkness, Looks had no difficulty in slipping past the convoy's escort screen and taking up a position slightly ahead and to port of the leading ships. From the conning tower he was just able to make out the ships in the port outside column, which was led by the 2,864-ton *Bristol City*, one of the few fully loaded ships in ONS 5. Down to her marks with a cargo of china clay and general, she was a tempting target, but Looks had his eye on bigger fish. Following in the wake of the British ship was the 5,565-ton US freighter *West Madaket*, in ballast and riding high out of the water, and astern of her again, J. & C. Harrison's 4,585-ton

Harperley labouring under a full cargo of coal from the Bristol Channel. If he missed her, then there were plenty of others in the background.

A few minutes after 2300 on 4 May, using the *West Madaket* as his central aiming point, Looks fired a spread of four from his bow tubes, then turned short about and sent another torpedo after them from his stern tube. He later wrote in his War Diary:

> I have a group of five steamers ahead of me, three at approximately 1,500 metres and two behind them at about 2,500 metres. At 0102 I launch two fan shots at the larger two of the three nearest ships, one launch of two eels from Tubes II and III at a 6,000-tonner and another launch of two from Tubes I and IV at a 5,000-tonner . . . I then turn hard-a-starboard and launch a fifth eel from the stern tube at a 4,500 GRT freighter. All five eels hit home. The first fan launch at the 6,000-tonner detonated after runs of one minute 22 seconds and one minute 26 seconds, one hitting amidships and the other 20 metres from the stern. Two high smoke columns can be seen. The second fan launch hits the 5,000-tonner at the same locations on the hull after runs of one minute 47 seconds and one minute 51 seconds. Again there are two high detonation columns. The single launch from Tube V hit the 4,500-tonner amidships under the funnel. There is a very high detonation column topped by a large mushroom cloud. I suspect that all three steamers will sink because of the good positioning of the hits. I take off as fast as I can. A destroyer heads toward me from the north at high speed. The steamers I hit shoot up white rockets.

With so many ships steaming in close proximity to each other, it should have been virtually impossible for Looks, firing five torpedoes in quick succession and at close range, not to have scored with all five. In fact, one of his torpedoes missed altogether, while the other four went home. First to be hit was not the primary target, the *West Madaket*, but her near relation *West Maximus*, also in ballast and directly behind her in Column 2. The other unfortunate recipient of Looks's torpedoes was the *Harperley*, the third ship of Column 1.

Looks later went into more detail:

> I torpedoed two ships each with two torpedoes and one
> of the ships after the explosion of the torpedoes another
> big explosion happened on board the ship, perhaps
> the boiler also exploded, and in our glasses during the
> dark night we could observe this ship was sinking very
> quickly. Then I turned around with the submarine to
> fire the stern torpedo but it had a malfunction and ran
> straight on the surface with a big, white shining wake.
> As it didn't run with the exact speed this torpedo passed
> the target ship behind the stern and came to the second
> column of the convoy and hit there another steamer, but
> I couldn't observe any result, just the explosion of the tor-
> pedo, because at that time one of the escort vessels cer-
> tainly picked me up and got contact with me so I was
> forced to submerge. This escort vessel depth charged
> me for some minutes and then joined the convoy. I had
> the chance to reload two of the bow torpedoes and after
> about one hour I surfaced and proceeded on the last bear-
> ing of the convoy and I was once more successful to get
> contact with the convoy and I did just the same as the
> time before. I proceeded on the port side of this convoy
> to a position where I had the chance to attack and once
> more was lucky by slipping through the gap between two
> of the escort vessels and closing to the port column of the
> convoy and both torpedoes hit the target ship and then
> the escort vessel was alerted and close in about one thou-
> sand metres distance and I had to disappear. I got once
> more depth charges for about one hour without hitting
> me but this happened just before dawn so I had no more
> chance to find the convoy during the darkness, and of
> course now we had the daylight coming up and I had to
> stay underwater for a longer time.

Since the opening of the attack on ONS 5 by the U-boats, Captain
Brooks in the *West Maximus* had taken the precaution of posting
extra lookouts and having his guns manned at all times. This
meant that dozens of pairs of eyes were continually scanning the
dark horizon for the first sign of danger. For all that, no one saw the
wake of U-264's torpedoes speeding towards the *West Maximus*.

If the American ship had been a knot faster, the torpedoes might have missed her, and no one would have been any the wiser. As it was, the first torpedo hit in her after peak ballast tank and all but blew her stern clean off. Seconds later, even before the muffled roar of the first explosion had died down, the second torpedo went home in No. 3 hold, just abaft the bridge. The blast demolished the watertight bulkhead between the hold and the engine room, and the sea poured in, flooding first the boiler room, then the engine space. The *West Maximus*, with her boiler fires extinguished and listing heavily to port, slewed to a halt.

A quick check on the visible damage was enough to convince Captain Brooks that she was in imminent danger of sinking, and he gave the order to abandon ship. With the list increasing by the minute, and the ship rolling drunkenly in the trough of the waves, the prospects for getting away were not good, but discipline and good seamanship prevailed. All four lifeboats were launched without mishap, and of the sixty-two men on board, all but six escaped. Seaman Gunner Lester Frey was drowned while trying to jump from a raft into a lifeboat, and five others, including Second Officer Michael Slaupas, were missing, believed killed when the torpedoes struck.

The *West Maximus* was still afloat after she had been abandoned, and Captain Brooks decided to keep the boats alongside in case there was a possibility of re-boarding when daylight came. It was a forlorn hope, for within half an hour the stricken ship rolled over and sank. Cold and wet, but otherwise none the worse for their ordeal, the survivors were picked up by HMS *Northern Spray* at about 0900 on the 5th.

It was developing into a good night for Hartwig Looks. Just sixty seconds after he had crippled the *West Maximus*, his second fan of two torpedoes slammed into the hull of the *Harperley*, third ship of ONS 5's port outside column.

The 4,585-ton *Harperley*, sister ship to the *Harbury*, sunk less than an hour before by Heinrich Hasenschar in U-628, was under the command of Captain Joseph Turgoose. Just two weeks earlier, he had been sailing as Chief Officer with Harrisons, and had it not been for the fearful toll of officers this war was exacting, that would have been his lot for many more years to come. Now, like a proud but anxious father, he rarely left the bridge of his first command.

The *Harperley*, a conventionally built north-east coast tramp, carried a total crew of forty-nine, composed of British officers, Indian ratings and seven DEMS gunners. She had loaded 6,005 tons of coal in Newport, Mon. which was consigned to Buenos Aires. This involved a passage of 7,600 miles, of which the Atlantic crossing constituted only a quarter, but by far the most dangerous part. And to add to the hazards she faced on the crossing, the *Harperley* had been allotted a station in the outer column of the convoy. From the moment of leaving the North Channel, Captain Turgoose had felt uncomfortably vulnerable, and from the time the first ship, the *McKeesport*, had been torpedoed, he had kept his crew at their action stations, with all guns manned day and night.

The *Harperley* mounted the usual armament, consisting of a 4-inch, a 12-pounder, four 20mm Oerlikons and two twin Marlins. On the face of it, she should have been a match for any attacker, but against the unseen U-boat she had no defence. Of course, she carried no radar, and not surprisingly, no one saw the low silhouette of U-264 as she approached from the west under the cover of darkness. The first and only indication of danger came when two torpedoes ripped open her hull plates. Captain Turgoose wrote in his report:

> At 2256 when in position 55° 00' N, 42° 58' W, whilst steaming at 7½ knots on a course 192° (approximately), we were struck by two torpedoes. The weather was overcast, visibility good but very dark, rough sea with heavy swell, SW wind force 5.
>
> Both torpedoes struck almost simultaneously on the port side, the first one in the vicinity of the engine-room, whilst the second torpedo struck in way of the fore-mast. The explosion was not very violent, and appeared to be more of a dull thud. I did not notice a flash, neither was there a column of water thrown up, although I later learned from survivors of another vessel that they saw a big flash. Neither the submarine, nor the track of the torpedoes was observed.
>
> I was in the wheel-house at the time, and was surprised to find that apparently there was practically no visible damage. Even the glass windows of the wheel-house

were unbroken, the only visible damage being that one of the port boats was destroyed and No. 4 raft had carried away. The ship listed very heavily to port, submerging the holes in ship's side, thus making it impossible to see the extent of the damage.

Owing to the heavy list I ordered 'abandon ship'. A W/T message was sent out, and the rockets fired, one of which failed to function. I endeavoured to ring the engine-room telegraph but found that it was jammed, although the engines must have stopped when the first torpedo struck as it was the first torpedo which flooded the engine-room and caused the deaths of the 2nd, 3rd and 4th Engineers. I did not consider there was sufficient time to put the boat's wireless set into a lifeboat so it was left behind.

The *Harperley* carried four lifeboats, two 36-man boats abaft the funnel and two smaller boats each with a capacity of sixteen on the lower bridge deck. She was also equipped with four large wooden liferafts stowed on ramps, two abreast the foremast and two at the mainmast. With a total complement of forty-nine on board, in normal circumstances this should have been more than adequate to allow an orderly evacuation. However, circumstances were far from normal on that night in the north Atlantic. One of the 36-man boats had been reduced to matchwood by the blast of the torpedoes, the weather was atrocious, the *Harperley*'s generator had failed and the ship was in complete darkness; on top of this, her heavy list to port complicated the whole sorry mess. In spite of all these disadvantages, the three remaining lifeboats were manned and launched, being clear of the ship in eight minutes.

Captain Turgoose, in one of the small bridge boats, had only four men with him, while the large boat, with his Second Officer in charge, was full to capacity with thirty-four men. The official ruling of the day for lifeboat capacity was 10 cubic feet per man, definitely not enough in which to swing the proverbial cat, and taking into account the extra gear carried in a ship's lifeboat in wartime, this boat was clearly overcrowded. To even things up, Turgoose transferred nine men to his boat, leaving the Second Officer with twenty-five, which at least gave sufficient room for the oars to be shipped.

Having solved that problem, Captain Turgoose discovered that the *Harperley*'s other small boat had capsized in the heavy seas and that twenty-three men were clinging to her upturned hull. These men were clearly in great danger, but Turgoose was unable to help them as he feared the two boats might be thrown together by the rough seas and smashed. The best he could do was reassure the men in the water that he would stand by them until help came.

It was not until the darkest hour before the dawn that HMS *Northern Spray* found them. Her commander, Lieutenant Francis Downer, described the rescue:

> At 0305Z a red light was sighted and we closed, but the light disappeared very shortly and after searching nothing was found. This may have been the wireless operators from S.S. HARPERLEY on an upturned boat. There was no sign of them when daylight came.
>
> At 0415Z further lights were seen and survivors were picked up off a raft from S.S. HARBURY and ten minutes later further survivors were picked up from one of the HARPERLEY'S boats from the HARBURY, HARPERLEY, and a US ship the WEST MAXIMUS. The HARBURY was still afloat as well.
>
> At 0455Z further lights were seen to the southward which turned out to be other survivors from the HARBURY, HARPERLEY, and a US ship the WEST MAXIMUS. The HARBURY was still afloat as well.
>
> Until 0800Z we were engaged in picking up survivors from boats and rafts which had spread out from each other.

The *Northern Spray*, an ex-Grimsby trawler of 620 tons gross, just 188ft long and 28ft in the beam, tiny in comparison with the merchantmen she was helping to protect, by then had on board a total of 143 survivors, some injured, all cold, wet and dripping black oil. Lieutenant Downer, himself an ex-merchant seaman, wrote in his log:

> I was beginning to wonder where to put others if there were any more, as the mess decks and ward room and all

cabins were jammed tight. The crew of HMS NORTHERN SPRAY slept on deck the first night. We have tried to muster as much clean clothing as we can find. The cook had to prepare nearly 200 dinners, he refused any help from some cook survivors saying, 'I don't want strangers in my galley', although the galley was quite inadequate. The survivors from the various ships turned to and cleaned the mess decks as best they could, without water, which is now rationed. The crew from the American vessel S.S. WEST MAXIMUS went up and cleaned the four-inch gun.

The majority of survivors on board the rescue trawler were Lascars, ratings from the two Harrison ships *Harbury* and *Harperley*, and while, as Lieutenant Downer noted, the American and British survivors did their best to help out in this crowded ship, the Indians refused to join in. In fact, one unnamed witness commented, 'The Lascars sat around on tables and would not move, drawing knives and threatening to use them. *Spray*'s commander formed an armed party to round them up and lock them in the chain locker.'

With 143 survivors on board in addition to her crew of twenty-seven, the *Northern Spray* was now so crowded as to be incapable of any useful action, so she was ordered to detach and make for St John's at all possible speed. She arrived safely on 8 May.

While the *Northern Spray* was busy pulling survivors from the water, on the far side of the convoy a sudden burst of star shell was lighting up the night sky. U-514 had arrived to add to the chaos already reigning.

U-514, a 1,120-ton U-cruiser, was on her third war patrol, having sailed from Lorient on 15 April. Under the command of 29-year-old Hans-Jürgen Auffermann, the Type IXC, built in Hamburg in 1941, had already made a name for herself by sinking six Allied merchantmen and damaging two others. Auffermann was hungry for more of the same.

U-514's current venture into the North Atlantic had not begun well. She had already been twice attacked by enemy aircraft, first by a Wellington of 172 Squadron RAF, then by a Whitley of 10 Squadron. As it happened, both attacks were unsuccessful, and the submarine had escaped unharmed, but happening so early in the voyage, they had an adverse effect on the morale of her crew. And now her run of bad luck was about to continue.

As she approached the leading ships of ONS 5, U-514 was picked up on radar by HMS *Vidette,* stationed 5,000yds on the convoy's starboard bow. The destroyer increased speed to 22 knots, and Lieutenant Commander Hart ran down the line of bearing. Within five minutes the surfaced U-boat was sighted.

The *Vidette* was less than 700yds off before Auffermann became aware of her creaming bow-wave as she bore down on him. U-514 was only seconds from being rammed when he cleared the conning tower and crash-dived. As U-514 sank below the surface in a welter of foam, *Vidette* ran over her, releasing a 14-charge pattern of depth charges set to shallow.

As his charges exploded with a dull roar, Hart turned to starboard under full helm, opened the range to 1,000yds, then stood off listening for an Asdic contact. There was no echoing ping. Ten, then twenty minutes went by, and still there was no contact, leading Hart to believe that the U-boat, her pressure hull blown open by his charges, had gone straight to the bottom. In fact, although U-514 had been severely battered, she was still very much alive, but her periscope was out of action, the stern gland of one of her propellers had sprung a serious leak and water was pouring into the boat. Although the leak was eventually plugged, U-514 was clearly in no condition to play any further part in the action against ONS 5. Auffermann contacted Lorient and was ordered to return to base.

After an hour had passed with nothing stirring below the surface, Lieutenant Commander Hart was about to abandon his vigil, when another small echo came up on *Vidette's* radar at 3,600yds. As before, Hart ran down the line of bearing and minutes later was rewarded by the sight of a surfaced U-boat. Heinz-Eberhard Müller in U-662 was about to join the party.

U-662, a Type VIIC, had set out from St Nazaire on 23 March and on her way west had already been involved in a pack attack on the northbound convoy SL 126. Oberleutnant Müller, on his first voyage in command, had celebrated his recent promotion by sinking two British ships totalling 13,011 tons and damaging another of 7,174 tons. This considerable achievement would lead to his early elevation to Kapitänleutnant; meanwhile, having tasted success, he was eager to get back into action.

Unfortunately for Heinz-Eberhard Müller, his early run of success was about to come to an abrupt end, for having, as he believed, put an end to U-514, Lieutenant Commander Hart had the bit between his teeth. Calling for full speed, he charged at the U-boat, at the same time opening fire on her conning tower with his 20mm Oerlikons.

Müller acted instinctively, presenting his stern to *Vidette* and running away at full speed. With the destroyer's tracers slicing past his conning tower, he was about to stop her onward rush with a torpedo from his stern tube when he realized he had left it too late. *Vidette* was by this time within 80yds of U-662, and the frothing of her bow wave indicated that she intended to ram.

At the last minute Müller cleared the conning tower, ordering main ballast to be flooded as he scrambled below, slamming the hatch after him. The avenging destroyer was almost on top of the submerging U-boat as she sank beneath the waves, and Hart followed her down with a pattern of fourteen depth charges set to shallow. And that – at least, it seemed to those on the open bridge of *Vidette* – was the end of U-662. But they were mistaken; although the charges exploded dangerously close to the U-boat they caused only superficial damage.

Shaken but intact, U-662 escaped into safer waters. However, *Vidette*'s depth charges were not entirely wasted. Unknown to Lieutenant Commander Hart, when he attacked U-662 another U-boat, said to be Claus-Peter Carlsen's U-732, was submerged nearby, and she had caught the full blast of the 14-charge pattern. She was then picked up by *Vidette*'s Asdic and was the target of another twelve depth charges. Grievously damaged, she was forced to retire from the fight and return to Brest for repairs.

The battle continued on the port quarter of the convoy, where the corvette *Snowflake* was standing guard. Her radar was showing a small echo at 3,000yds, but although the area was illuminated with star shell, nothing was visible to the eye. Minutes later, *Snowflake*'s hydrophones detected the hiss of a compressed air release, indicative of a torpedo being fired at close range. If it was a torpedo, it must have missed the corvette by a wide margin, but the noise convinced Lieutenant Chesterman that he had intercepted another U-boat. This was confirmed when his Asdic operator reported a firm echo on the port bow at 300yds. Putting the echo right ahead, Chesterman increased to full speed, dropping a 10-charge pattern as the corvette surged ahead. The exploding charges produced no result other than knocking *Snowflake*'s Asdic out of action and thus ending the pursuit. The unidentified U-boat was later reported to be Hartwig Looks' U-264.

After a long spell in port for repairs and maintenance, U-264 returned to the North Atlantic and continued to operate against Allied convoys, but without further success. When she sailed out of St Nazaire on her fifth war patrol in February 1944, Hartwig Looks was still in command and more than ever determined to end the boat's continued run of bad luck. His orders were specific: U-264 was to join with nineteen other U-boats in a search for the westbound convoy ON 224. This was reported to consist of eighty Allied merchantmen scheduled to load arms and supplies in America for the planned invasion of the Continent. The intention was to sink as many ships as possible while they were still westbound.

U-264 made contact with ON 224 on 18 February and ran into trouble at once, being heavily depth charged by the convoy's escorts. She escaped with only minor damage but later fell foul of the Second Support Group, under the command of the sub-killer supreme, Captain Johnny Walker, which had been despatched to the convoy's aid.

Captain Walker's sloops lived up to their reputation, literally blowing U-264 out of the water with a deluge of 150 depth charges. On the surface and unable to dive, U-264 came under fire from the British sloops, but apart from several slightly wounded men, Hartwig Looks and his entire crew of fifty-one abandoned ship in good order. They were all picked up by the Support Group and taken prisoner, while U-264 was pounded into a sinking wreck by Walker's guns.

CHAPTER TWELVE

The Stragglers

As a pale grey dawn broke over the troubled ocean, the number of U-boats involved in the attack on ONS 5 was growing by the hour. The latest to arrive was the Danzig-built Type VIIC U-413. In her conning tower was 26-year-old Kapitänleutnant Gustav Poel, who had commanded her from the day she was commissioned in the late summer of 1942. Poel, who had joined the Kriegsmarine in 1936, although still young, was a man of wide experience. He had served in the light cruiser *Emden* and the E-boat *Tiger*, seeing action in the Spanish Civil War with the latter. He had also spent time ashore on the staff of BdU in Kiel, and as liaison officer to the Italian Submarine Command in Bordeaux. His command of U-413 had begun auspiciously with the sinking of the 20,000-ton British liner *Warwick Castle* in November 1942, but this proved to be a false dawn; in the months that followed Poel could lay claim to only two Allied merchantmen, amounting to less than 9,000 tons between them.

Gustav Poel sailed from Brest on his third war patrol with U-413 on 29 March 1943 intent on adding to his meagre score, and already his determination to shine was showing results. Following orders to join those boats already operating in waters south of Greenland, U-413 was just three weeks out from Brest when she came across the British steamer *Wanstead* drifting in the wake of Convoy ONS 3. The *Wanstead*, bound from the Tyne to New York in ballast, had been torpedoed earlier by U-415 and abandoned by her crew, so it had been a simple matter for Poel to finish her off, thereby laying claim to another 5,486 tons of Allied shipping.

Continuing southwards, U-413 had received orders to join in the attack on ONS 5. She sighted the convoy in the early hours of 5 May, and Poel moved in eagerly to select a suitable target. Having already lost five ships to the U-boats, and with four others detached some 80 miles astern under the sole protection of the corvette *Pink*, ONS 5 was in considerable disarray. Seeing this, Poel may have been less than careful as he made his approach to the ships.

Hot from the pursuit of another U-boat, believed to be Hartwig Looks' U-264, the Flower-class corvette *Loosestrife*, under the command of Lieutenant Herbert Stonehouse, detected U-413 by radar as she approached the port side of the convoy. A few minutes later, the U-boat was visible by eye, and *Loosestrife* opened fire with her 4-inch and followed up with her port and starboard Oerlikons, spraying U-413's conning tower with 120 rounds of 20mm. Numerous hits were scored, although no real damage was done, and Gustav Poel wisely dived without attempting to return fire. Stonehouse then waded in with a pattern of nine depth charges lobbed into the whirlpool left by the submerging boat. *Loosestrife* claimed a 'likely kill', but in fact U-413 again sustained only superficial damage. Poel later denied that the corvette scored any hits on his boat and wrote of the corvette's depth charges in his log: 'Heavy tremors in the boat, damage is slight, everything can be repaired immediately, except for the main transmitter. Everyone breathes a sigh of relief.'

While *Loosestrife* was occupied with U-413, Kapitänleutnant Rolf Manke in U-358 had made a silent approach from the east. The Type VIIC, commissioned by the then Oberleutnant Manke in Flensburg in August 1942, had left St Nazaire three weeks earlier on her second war patrol, and although she had been shadowing ONS 5 for some days she was yet to become involved. As he made his stealthy approach to the convoy, Manke noted that he could see 'at least ten lifeboats with lights floating about', presumably from ships recently sunk.

Trimmed right down, U-358 was able to approach unseen in the half light. Running at full speed, she was quite easily able to overtake the two ships remaining in the port outside column of the convoy, the 2,864-ton *Bristol City* leading, followed by the 5,138-ton *Temple Arch*. The latter was by far the more tempting target, being almost twice the size of the leader, but Manke chose the smaller ship, largely because he believed she had slowed down and was about to stop to pick up survivors from the lifeboats he had seen. The *Bristol City* was actually steaming at 6½ knots, which was the convoy speed at the time. Approaching to within 1,500 metres, Manke fired a fan of two torpedoes from his bow tubes. He described the result in his War Diary:

Two explosions were heard in the boat after 113 seconds run, so perhaps both torpedoes hit. A violent explosion could be seen amidships. The steamer broke apart in the middle and sank within one minute. Because of the vessel's length (150m) and its 5½ hatches, I judge the steamer to be 8,000 GRT. According to Gröner, she belongs to the Port Hardy class (8,700 GRT).

Rolf Manke's gross overestimation of the *Bristol City*'s tonnage is puzzling, but she turned out to be a wise choice of target, being one of the few fully loaded ships in the convoy. Owned by Charles Hill & Son of Bristol, she was described as a 'sturdy Western Ocean boat' and was carrying 2,500 tons of china clay from Fowey, plus a small amount of general cargo, all destined for New York. In command was Captain Arthur Llewellyn Webb, and her total complement was forty-four, which included six DEMS gunners. She was armed with a 4-inch, two Oerlikons, three twin Marlins and a Lewis gun. At the time she was torpedoed, all guns were manned and her crew were all at their action stations – not that it did her any good. Captain Webb described what happened in his report:

> There was a heavy confused swell, with a S.W. wind force 5. The weather was overcast, it was very dark, but visibility was good.
>
> No one saw the track of the torpedo, which struck in No. 4 hold on the port side. The explosion was dull, much quieter than I would have expected. I saw a flash, and a huge column of water was thrown into the air, which cascaded down and flooded the decks. The port lifeboat and after rafts were destroyed by the explosion. The main topmast collapsed, and the engine room flooded rapidly. I rang down from the bridge and ordered the engines to be stopped. A large amount of debris was scattered about the deck, so it was impossible to see details of the deck damage.

While Captain Webb was recovering from the shock of the sudden attack on his ship, Rolf Manke followed up with a second torpedo, which slammed into the *Bristol City*'s No. 1 hold and exploded with catastrophic results. An eruption of china clay mixed with water and debris soared high in the air and fell back, coating the foredeck and bridge with a dirty grey sludge. At the same time, the fore topmast snapped off and fell to the deck, its tangled rigging adding to the chaos. When the air cleared, it could be seen that the windlass had been blown clean off the forecastle head, the hatchboards and tarpaulins of the forward holds had been stripped and one of the liferafts stowed abreast the foremast had disappeared into the night. Further aft, the wireless cabin abaft the bridge had collapsed under the force of the blast. First Radio Officer John Kennedy and Second Radio Officer John Thomas, who were manning the radio at the time, both lost their lives.

The *Bristol City*, that 'sturdy Western Ocean boat', slowed to a halt with the sea pouring into her holds through the holes blasted in her hull fore and aft. She was settling bodily at an alarming rate, and Captain Webb had no other option but to order his crew into the boats. He described what happened next:

> The boat's wireless set was kept in the chart room, but it had to be left behind owing to lack of time. A ship in the next column sent up rockets for us, as we did not fire any, nor did we send out a wireless signal. Within eight minutes, one lifeboat was lowered, and some twenty men jumped into it from the deck. I was waist deep in water as I left the ship, which had settled by the head and was steaming under. Nine minutes after the first torpedo struck, the ship disappeared.
>
> A jolly boat was lowered with five men in it; it capsized on becoming waterborne, throwing its occupants into the sea. Two of these were drowned, but the remaining three men managed to struggle to a raft. We eventually took these three men into the lifeboat, and picked up four others from the water. All the crew were wearing their lifejackets with the red lights, and these greatly facilitated the rescue work.

After drifting at the mercy of wind and sea for just over an hour, the *Bristol City*'s lifeboat was sighted by HMS *Loosestrife*, and Captain Webb and twenty-six other survivors were taken on board. Two more men were later found in the water, cold, exhausted, but still alive.

Immediately after putting the second torpedo into the *Bristol City*, Manke lined up his sights on the next ship astern, the 5,565-ton

US-flag *West Madaket*, and fired a single torpedo, but due to a technical fault on the part of the U-boat, the American ship survived. Manke noted in his War Diary:

> Launch order given, but the torpedo stuck in the tube. A *Mechanikersmaat* [engineer's mate] prodded it out with a mine ejector and it hit the target after a run of 118 seconds. A large explosion resulted amidships on the target and the steamer broke apart and sank in a matter of seconds. From Gröner we judged the vessel to be of the Clan Macnab class, 6,000 GRT . . . Only a destroyer and another escort could now be seen. We pursued the convoy, whose position was obvious from the frequent shooting of flares, but then, because of the sea force and swell, we dived in order to reload in a stable environment.

The torpedo intended for the *West Madaket*, due to the delay in launching, had run on through the first and second columns of ONS 5 to score a random hit on the third ship of Column 3, the 5,512-ton British steamer *Wentworth*. Owned by the Dalgleish Steam Shipping Company, the Newcastle-registered *Wentworth* was under the command of Captain Reginald Phillips and carried a crew of forty-six, including six DEMS gunners. Bound for New York in ballast, her ultimate destination was Cuba, where she was scheduled to pick up a cargo of sugar.

At about 0230 on the 5th, all having been quiet since the torpedoing of the *Harperley*, Captain Phillips had decided to go below for a much needed break, but he had not been in his cabin for many minutes when the bridge telephone rang to report that the *Bristol City* had been hit. Phillips was back on the bridge of the *Wentworth* within seconds, and five minutes after he entered the wheelhouse, U-358 struck again. Phillips wrote in his report:

> At 0310 on 5th May in position 53° 59'N 43° 55'W, steaming at 6 knots on a course 220° (approx.), we were struck by a torpedo. The weather was cloudy but clear, it was just dark, and visibility was good. There was a moderate sea and swell and light variable airs.
>
> The torpedo struck on the port side, midships, in the stokehold. It was not a loud explosion, there was no flash or flame, and only a very small amount of water was

thrown up. The funnel collapsed, the wireless room also collapsed, and all electricity failed. The main deck was split across midships, the port shell plates were cracked, and there was a hole in the ship's side about 12 feet in diameter, extending about 3 feet above the waterline.

When the *Wentworth* staggered under the blast of Rolf Manke's torpedo, the Radio Officer on watch followed standard procedure by sending out a prearranged SOS to all ships, but this went no further than his Morse key. As in most merchant ships of the day, the *Wentworth*'s wireless aerial was suspended between her masts, and it had been brought down by the explosion. Furthermore, the distress rockets on the bridge could not be fired as they were jammed fast in their sockets. As a result, no one other than those in the ships close by was aware that the *Wentworth* had been torpedoed.

Captain Phillips' report continues:

> The Third Engineer, who was on watch, stopped the engines immediately and made his escape through the tunnel escape, so it was lucky for him that the watertight door was open. I ordered the boats to be lowered and went down to the lower bridge to superintend the lowering of the starboard boat. The two bunker derricks had fallen on the falls of this boat, but after some difficulty we were able to clear them, the boat was lowered and drifted away with one man in it. The remainder of the crew of this boat rushed to the boat deck. I went over to the port motor boat on the boat deck, lowered it, and gave the crew orders to stand by alongside and wait for me. By 0330 all four boats were in the water and three of them were clear of the ship. I went forward and tried to release the forward raft, but the slipping gear had jammed and I could not release it. The ship began cracking up so at 0350 I decided it was time to abandon. When I left the ship in the port motor boat it was broad daylight. I found that a few of the crew had jumped over the side and had been picked up by other boats with the exception of the Assistant Steward who could not be found. The remainder of the missing men were in the engine room or stokehold when the explosion occurred.

At 0400 I sighted a corvette not far away. I signalled to her with a torch which she acknowledged and shortly afterwards she steamed over. By 0530 we were all on board HMS *Loosestrife*. The Captain asked me what happened to the Confidential Books, and learning that they were still on board he steamed along the port side of the Wentworth and fired a depth charge which landed close to the ship's side. He then steamed round on the starboard side and put two shells into No. 2 hold, the ship was still afloat at 0600 when I went below, but at 0700 the Captain sent down to inform me that she had sunk.

As the *Wentworth* slipped below the waves, aboard HMS *Tay* reports were flooding in of enemy submarines threatening the convoy. HF/DF bearings, radar and Asdic contacts indicated that at least seven U-boats were attempting to penetrate the thin defensive screen provided by Sherwood and his remaining escorts. The situation was in fact far more serious than it appeared at first sight. Later records show that the total number of U-boats threatening ONS 5 was the greatest ever to be deployed against one convoy. This was confirmed in mid-morning, when Sherwood ordered Lieutenant Commander Ingram in HMS *Oribi* to investigate HF/DF bearings at 12 miles on the port bow of the convoy. After steaming for 45 minutes at 16 knots, *Oribi* sighted a smoke haze low on the horizon which looked suspiciously like the exhausts of a U-boat motoring on the surface. Ingram increased speed to 30 knots, and very soon a conning tower was visible, confirming his suspicions. Then, as *Oribi* raced in to attack, a second U-boat was seen, and a few minutes later, a third. All three U-boats were moving away from the convoy in line abreast and at full speed.

This was a golden opportunity for *Oribi*, but before she was able to bring her guns into action, all three U-boats crash-dived. Ingram at once reduced speed to 15 knots and began an Asdic sweep. This immediately produced a firm echo at 800yds, clearly identified as 'submarine drawing left'. To Ingram's surprise, the echo was closing rapidly, the submerged U-boat now obviously on an opposite course to the destroyer. As it passed down the *Oribi*'s port side it ran into a pattern of four depth charges dropped squarely in its path. This apparently had no effect, as contact was regained a few minutes later. Ingram gave chase at full speed, dropping another ten charges when passing over the U-boat. These produced a heavy underwater explosion and a huge upwelling of water. Lookouts then reported a periscope emerging from the disturbed water astern and moving away at speed. *Oribi* came around under full helm, a pattern of five charges rolling off her stern as she gave chase. These seemed to have no effect on the U-boat, and as *Oribi's* stock of depth charges was running low, Ingram decided to call it a day and return to the convoy. He briefly noted the action in his log:

> 1249. Following on the explosion of the charges, and slightly less than two minutes after the first charge was fired, two unexplained explosions were heard, one heavy and one of less intensity, resulting in a large visible eruption of air. It was reported from the quarterdeck that a periscope was sighted for a moment in the middle of the disturbance caused by the depth charge pattern, moving slowly to port. Among those who are certain that they saw this was Mr Stacey, Gunner (T), but it was not observed from the bridge.

Later reports showed that *Oribi* had flushed out not three, but four U-boats, namely U-223, U-231, U-621 and U-634, which had come together with the intention of mounting a combined attack on ONS 5. None of these boats received any significant damage from Ingram's prolonged depth charging, but their planned attack had been frustrated by *Oribi's* intervention.

Having stirred up a hornet's nest by torpedoing the *Bristol City* and the *Wentworth* in quick succession, Rolf Manke took U-358 away to the north to seek quieter waters in which to reload his tubes. Some six hours later, while the boat was hove-to on the surface, her lookouts sighted smoke on the horizon ahead. This proved to come from the funnels of four stragglers from ONS 5, the British ships *Director* and *Dunsley*, the Norwegian-flag *Gudvor* and the American *West Madaket*, all proceeding under the protection of the corvette HMS *Pink*. By now they had fallen 80 miles astern of the main convoy and were steaming in line abreast, with *Pink* zig-zagging ahead of them.

In command of HMS *Pink* was 27-year-old Lieutenant Robert Atkinson RNR, DSC. An experienced ex-Merchant Navy officer,

Atkinson was a graduate of the Anti-Submarine Warfare School at Portland and already had one U-boat kill to his credit. Whilst commanding the corvette *Rhododendron* in 1941 he had sunk U-104, and since then had commanded three other corvettes in the North Atlantic. Rolfe Manke was about to meet his match.

U-358 had by this time gone to periscope depth and was approaching Atkinson's small convoy on its starboard side, intent on making a quick hit-and-run attack. The plan had to be abandoned when, at 2,200yds, U-358 was caught in *Pink's* Asdic beam. Lieutenant Atkinson recorded in his log:

> At 0954, a first-class contact was obtained bearing 310, 2,200 yards, which was immediately classified as submarine. The a/s conditions were splendid, the echoes being by far the cleanest and sharpest I have ever heard.

Pink's commander was now faced with a challenging decision: should he hold back and defend his charges, or should he meet the U-boat head-on? Any attack would involve full speed manoeuvring, which would make serious inroads into the corvette's already depleted fuel supply. The activity of the past few days had left her with only 30 per cent of her bunker capacity, and with the main convoy being so far ahead, there was little prospect of being able to replenish her tanks from one of the fleet tankers with ONS 5. Atkinson deliberated only for a few moments, then decided to adhere to the Royal Navy's rule of thumb, which is that the best form of defence is attack. He called for full speed ahead.

The water threshed under *Pink's* stern as she surged forward, running in to drop a 3-charge pattern directly over the shadowing U-boat. Asdic contact was regained as soon as the disturbance caused by the exploding depth charges settled. Bearing and distance indicated that U-358 was going deeper and attempting to escape to the east. *Pink* followed, dropping a pattern of ten charges as she caught up with and ran over the fleeing submarine. Again, Atkinson listened in vain for breaking-up noises underwater, but there was nothing but the steady returning Asdic ping from the target. In desperation, he ordered the forward-firing Hedgehog to open fire, but the notoriously fickle weapon chose that moment to malfunction.

Atkinson reverted to depth charges, which now rained down on U-358 as she twisted and turned in an effort to shake off her determined attacker. Two ten-charge patterns were dropped, the first set to 250 and 385ft, the second to 350 and 550ft. The exploding charges brought three huge air bubbles to the surface but no wreckage, and again no breaking-up noises were heard. Frustrated, Atkinson brought the corvette short round under full helm and ordered the Hedgehog crew to try again. This time, the twenty-four 65lb spigot mortars soared through the air, only to explode on hitting the water. Another wasted effort.

While Lieutenant Atkinson was engrossed in hunting down the U-boat, his charges, the four merchant stragglers, had been steaming determinedly south, and were now 10 miles ahead of *Pink* and dangerously exposed. It was time for their escorting corvette to rejoin them, but Robert Atkinson had the bit firmly between his teeth and was reluctant to give up the chase. He decided to make one last attempt to sink his quarry. Asdic contact had been re-established, and *Pink* raced in to drop another pattern of ten charges, eight of which were set to 350 and 550ft, the other two to 700ft.

When the depth charges had rolled over *Pink's* stern, Atkinson hauled the corvette out to starboard and listened for what he hoped would be the death throes of the U-boat. Once more he listened in vain. When the rumble of the exploding charges had subsided, all that could be heard was the silence of the sea. Disappointed, short on fuel, and now with a much depleted stock of depth charges, Atkinson reluctantly decided to abandon the hunt and return to his convoy. He recorded in his log:

> Course was set to rejoin, 240-15 knots, my convoy now being some ten miles ahead. At 1139, a dull and most powerful underwater explosion shook the ship, low in note and like a deep grunt. Initial surprise was felt on board, but it was recognized immediately to be a deep underwater explosion some distance off. I can only think that this was the submarine, or some part of it, exploding astern deep down, and I consider this to have been the case. I was sorely tempted to turn back and steam to the area of the attack to look for complete evidence of destruction, but this was considered not prudent, with five merchant

ships ahead some eight miles (one had joined in the fore-
noon) and unprotected as they now had been for an hour
and a half. I therefore dismissed the idea and continued to
rejoin at full speed. At 1253 my worst fears materialised . . .

In the hour and a half *Pink* was away from her convoy, it had
been joined by a fifth straggler from ONS 5, the 5,666-ton British
steamer *Yearby*, which had once been the leading ship of the
convoy's Column 10. Engine problems had led to her dropping
further and further astern, until she came under Atkinson's protection. Unwittingly, the *Yearby* had brought with her an unwelcome follower, U-584.

U-584, a Type VIIC under the command of 31-year-old Kapitänleutnant Joachim Deecke, was six weeks out from Brest and had
yet to take part in the attack on ONS 5. Having now chanced
upon what appeared to be a soft target, five merchantmen steaming at 8½ knots and with no escort, Deecke wasted no time, closing in from port and firing a spread of two torpedoes at the outer
ship of the line. She was the American steamer *West Madaket* of
5,565 tons.

Like her late sister *West Maximus*, the *West Madaket* was a typical American tramp. Built in the dying months of the First World
War as a commercial cargo carrier, she had been requisitioned
by the US Navy as a supply ship. She made only two voyages
to Europe before the war ended, was then decommissioned and,
like her sister ship, spent the next twenty-three years laid up in a
backwater in the Gulf of Mexico. The call came for her to return
to sea when America again went to war in Europe in December
1942, and she was then brought back into service under the
management of the Waterman Steamship Company of Mobile.
Commanded by Captain Hans Schroder, she was manned by a
crew of sixty, which included an Armed Guard detachment of
twenty-two who came with her armament of one 4-inch, one
3-inch and six Oerlikons.

HMS *Pink* was within 3 miles of rejoining her convoy and
steaming as fast as her flashing pistons would take her. On her
bridge, Lieutenant Robert Atkinson, binoculars glued to his eyes,
urged her on with a silent prayer. But the gods were not listening.
As he watched, a huge column of smoke and flame erupted from
the *West Madaket,* and she fell out of the line.

Captain Hans Schroder wrote in his report:

> A sudden jar was felt at that time and a heavy geyser of
> water was seen by the Officer of the Watch and several
> members of the crew on the port quarter. The vessel
> immediately started settling by the stern and a large crack
> in the deck plating was observed amidships, port side. A
> hole 2½ft by 5ft was seen on the starboard side, and it is
> believed there was a larger hole on the port side below
> the waterline. The after deck became awash abaft No.
> 5 hatch and the steering gear went out of order. A blue
> smoke came through the shaft alley into the engine room.
> Engines were secured at once.

After receiving damage reports which indicated that the *West
Madaket*'s back was broken, Captain Schroder gave the order to
abandon ship. Three lifeboats were launched, and all sixty-one on
board left the ship without incident. They were picked up by HMS
Pink three quarters of an hour later.

Lieutenant Atkinson takes up the story:

> I dropped charges intermittently to keep the U-boat down;
> I stopped to pick up the survivors . . . At 1405, I sank the
> wreck with the two starboard throwers set to 50 feet. She
> split in two and sank leaving no trace, which surprised
> me, as she had some 540 tons of oil bunkers on board at
> the time of sinking . . . At 1530, PINK was again in station
> having collected the four remaining ships, DUNSLEY,
> DIRECTOR, YEARBY and Norwegian GUDVOR.
> YEARBY had joined that morning just before noon. At
> 1630 a firm a/s contact was obtained at 1,000 yards ahead
> of the convoy, which was counter attacked at 1653 with
> 5 charges set to 150 feet. It is pointed out that 43 depth
> charges had been expended that morning during the hunt,
> 15 had been dropped at other times, leaving 21 remaining.
> My future commitments were unknown and therefore
> 5 charge patterns were considered to be the wisest policy.
> This contact was depth charged some 300 yards ahead of
> the second ship from the left, there being four ships in line

abreast. Some confusion was seen among them but their behaviour was excellent. One ran over the depth charge disturbance. Contact was not immediately gained in the wakes and this time I was more than anxious to regain station without delay. Further attacks were expected and station ahead was resumed immediately.

CHAPTER THIRTEEN

Drumbeat

ONS 5, now reduced to twenty-six ships sailing in ten columns abreast at 6½ knots, was some 450 miles east-north-east of Belle Isle and within less than three days steaming of Newfoundland waters. The weather, although still heavily overcast, had improved considerably, the wind having dropped to force 4 from the west, and the sea was no more than a moderate chop. Only the restless Atlantic swell told of the gales past, and there was a growing feeling in the convoy that they were 'home and dry'. Admiral Dönitz, monitoring the progress of his U-boats from his chateau overlooking the river at Kerneval, was of a similar mind. In the course of the morning he sent the following signal to his packs still hovering on the periphery of ONS 5:

> Immediately after nightfall the drumbeat must be timed to begin. Hurry – there are 40 of you – otherwise you will lose the convoy. The battle can't last long since the sea space left is short, so use every opportunity to the fullest with all your might.

Despite all the favourable signs, the convoy's S.O.E, Lieutenant Commander Robert Sherwood, scouting ahead in the frigate *Tay*, was not about to relax his vigilance. Radar and Asdic echoes and HF/DF bearings flooding in from all sides confirmed that the enemy had certainly not gone away. There were, as Dönitz had stated in his signal, still at least forty U-boats in the vicinity of ONS 5, all ready and eager to strike whenever the opportunity arose. It was just as well that the moderating weather had allowed *Tay* and the two destroyers *Offa* and *Oribi* to refuel from the fleet oiler *British Lady*. The third destroyer, HMS *Vidette*, having a greater fuel capacity, would be able to carry on for another twenty-four hours at least. The corvettes *Loosestrife*, *Snowflake* and *Sunflower*, with their miserly fuel consumption, would be there until the end.

Meanwhile, on the convoy's starboard bow, *Vidette* was busy depth charging another Asdic contact with similar results, while the other escorts were desperately trying to hold the defensive ring around ONS 5. For the moment, they appeared to be keeping the enemy at bay, but it could be only a matter of time before the U-boats made the breakthrough they were seeking.

Sailing at the head of the convoy's Column 2, and witness to this sudden rush of activity, was the 5,507-ton twin-screw motor vessel *Dolius*, one of the few elite cargo liners with ONS 5. She had been through it all before just two months earlier while with the ill-fated SC 122, and the memories of that one-sided battle were still fresh.

The *Dolius*, built on the Clyde in 1924, was one of Liverpool-based Alfred Holt's prestigious Blue Funnel Line, which between the wars had carried the best of British manufactured goods to the far corners of the Empire, returning home loaded with the bounteous wealth of the East. She was a true descendant of the legendary East Indiamen. Commanded by Captain Gilbert Cheetham, she was manned by a complement of seventy, made up of British officers and deck ratings, Chinese catering and engine room crew and nine DEMS gunners. She was a rare type of hybrid, driven by steam-assisted diesel engines, a combination of internal combustion and steam which produced a considerable saving in fuel.

When, a few days earlier, the *McKeesport* had been torpedoed by U-258, the *Dolius* had narrowly escaped a similar fate. In the midst of a blinding snow storm the track of a torpedo was seen crossing the British ship's stern, missing her by less than 25yds. This may have been one of the spread fired by U-258, or it could have come from one of the many other U-boats then taking advantage of the poor visibility to join in the attack. Weather conditions at the time were so bad that no one really knew where the torpedo came from, but although it missed his ship by a safe margin, Captain Cheetham had taken this as fair warning, and the *Dolius* had been on a state of high alert ever since.

It had been a long night for Cheetham, who had not left the bridge of the *Dolius* for a moment since the sun went down on the 4th. Now, with the weather moderating and the U-boats apparently retired for the time being, he decided to take advantage of the lull, however temporary, to go below to his cabin. War or no war, the routine business of the ship had to go on. There was a mountain of paperwork to deal with – and a mug of tea, hot and strong, would not go amiss.

The lull lasted longer than Captain Cheetham had anticipated. He found time not only to write several letters, but to drink his tea and have a quick splash in the sink. Very much refreshed, he returned to the bridge, unaware that danger was close at hand.

U-638, a Type VIIC commissioned in Hamburg in September 1942 by the then Oberleutnant Oskar Staudinger, had sailed from La Pallice fifteen days earlier with Staudinger, now Kapitänleutnant, in command again after a spell on shore. Her passage out to Cape Farewell had been uneventful, very much a continuation of her uneventful career to date. Although some seven months on active service, U-638 had still to play a significant part in the war; not one Allied ship had yet fallen to her torpedoes or shells. Approaching ONS 5 from the east, undetected so far and in perfect weather conditions for a submerged attack, Oskar Staudinger was determined to put an end to his boat's run of bad luck.

Cautious by nature and unwilling to linger longer than absolutely necessary, Staudinger approached as close to the convoy as he deemed prudent, then fired a spread of four torpedoes from his bow tubes into the ships without aiming at any particular target.

It had been a busy morning in the *Dolius'* engine room, with a squad of Chinese day workers carrying out essential maintenance under the critical eye of Second Engineer Bob Hutchinson. At precisely 1030, following the time-honoured practice in British merchant ships, the day workers had downed tools and trooped up on deck for their morning mug of tea and a cigarette. Left below were only the men of the watch, Fourth Engineer Samuel Parr, Junior Engineer Donald McGillivray and Greaser Lau Hing. All three died when Oskar Staudinger's torpedo slammed into the ship's side and the sea came cascading into the engine room. Young Donald McGillivray died not knowing that, just twelve hours earlier, his elder brother John had lost his life in the engine room of the *Harperley*.

Captain Cheetham described the torpedoing of the *Dolius* in his report:

> No-one saw the track of the torpedo which struck in the after part of the engine room on the starboard side. There was a dull explosion, but no flash was seen. No. 3 lifeboat was completely destroyed, and I saw a hole in the ship's starboard side measuring about 30ft long, extending

15/16ft above the water line. The force of the explosion stopped the engines, and the engine room flooded immediately. Later, when I tried to make an inspection of the damage, I could only get as far as the top platform, and looking down it appeared to me as if the engines had been shifted a couple of feet to port. No. 4 bulkhead collapsed, and No. 4 hold flooded. The after bulkhead in No. 4 hold was severely strained, I could hear water trickling into No. 5 hold, and I think this bulkhead also collapsed eventually. The hatches of No. 4 hold were blown off, as were the locking bars of No. 5 hatches. The vessel listed slightly, but quickly came upright again and settled by the stern.

Immediately after the explosion I gave orders to stand by the lifeboats. Some of the Chinese crew, in a momentary panic, rushed one of the lifeboats and commenced lowering it, but when I shouted to them, they stopped and later seemed to have got over their fright as they all behaved very well.

Captain Cheetham, having satisfied himself that his ship was beyond saving, made a thorough inspection of the decks and accommodation but could find no one lying injured. He gave the order to abandon ship, and the three remaining lifeboats were lowered to the water and boarded. They then cast off and pulled away from the sinking ship.

The boats were some distance from the ship when a man appeared on the upper deck of the *Dolius* and began waving his arms frantically. One of the boats put back to investigate, and the ship was re-boarded. It was then found that the stranded man was one of the DEMS ratings, who had been trapped in the gunners' quarters when the torpedo hit. Another gunner, Able Seaman Stanley Benit, was still missing. He was eventually found pinned under some wreckage, unconscious and severely injured. Both rescued men were lowered into the waiting lifeboat, which then pulled clear. As they left the ship's side, the boat's crew saw that the after deck of the *Dolius* was already awash.

The survivors were fortunate in that they were picked up within the half hour by the corvette *Sunflower*, which had dropped back in answer to their radioed call for help. Sadly, by this time the injured gunner Stanley Benit had died.

Witnesses to the torpedoing of the *Dolius* in nearby ships spoke of a loud explosion when she was hit, with a cloud of dirty black smoke mushrooming up from her after deck. Captain John Gates, commanding the *Baron Graham* in Column 3, said, 'As we steamed past the *Dolius* I looked through the gaping hole in her side and was amazed that a ship with such a gash in her could stay afloat without a list for so long.'

The *Dolius* was a typically stout Clyde-built ship, and she bore witness to the skill of her builders by staying afloat for several hours after she was torpedoed. As she drifted astern of the convoy she was taken under the wing of the American auxiliary USS *Manhasset*, which appeared to have attached herself to ONS 5.

The *Manhasset* was a dual-purpose auxiliary. She was part of a North Atlantic weather patrol and carried an array of meteorological instruments with which she gathered vital weather information intended to compile forecasts for the invasion of Europe, now just over a year away. At the same time, the *Manhasset*, based in Argentia, Newfoundland and Boston, Massachusetts, hunted for marauding German submarines. Just over a week earlier, she had detected and depth charged a suspect U-boat to the south of Cape Farewell, but with no positive result. However, the mere fact that this American auxiliary was patrolling their hunting grounds must have been more than just a nuisance to the U-boats.

The *Manhasset* was forced to abandon the *Dolius* when her sonar detected a U-boat lurking underwater in the vicinity. The auxiliary made six depth charge attacks, during the course of which she sighted the wake of a periscope and an oil slick, but no wreckage was seen. The identity of the U-boat was unknown, but it is believed it was at least damaged. As for the *Dolius*, left to her own devices she drifted out of sight and was not seen again. Presumably, she sank later in the day.

When the *Dolius* was torpedoed by U-638, HMS *Sunflower*, under the command of Acting Lieutenant Commander James Plomer RCNVR, was stationed on the port bow of ONS 5. She immediately reversed course and ran back between Columns 2 and 3 at emergency full speed. As she did so she picked up an Asdic contact at 1,200yds in the centre of the columns and slightly astern of the torpedoed ship. The contact, being extremely difficult to hold on to, was identified as almost certainly a submarine. With his most experienced operator at the Asdic, Plomer went in to attack, dropping a 10-charge pattern set to 150ft as the corvette passed over the target. He made the following entry in his log at the time:

> Throw-off and timing of the pattern are judged to have been correct. Pattern was dropped by voicepipe orders as buzzers had been out of action for some time. Contact could not then be regained. *Tay* closed the area but could not regain contact either. The position of the U-boat is confirmed by the captain of the *Dolius*, who considers that the torpedo was fired from close range; his reasons being the position of the other ships, the torpedo tracks not being seen, and the accuracy of the shot.

It was unfortunate that *Sunflower* had lost her head of steam as a result of her high-speed dash and was slow in running clear of the exploding charges. She was caught in the blast and received a severe shaking, which resulted in a cracked casting in her engine room; the gyro compass was knocked out and the Asdic set temporarily disabled. Lieutenant Commander Plomer's report of the incident continues:

> 1120–1200. Swept in vicinity of wreck, and when given permission to 'save' picked up survivors. Snowflake arrived to screen. One boat was sent back to pick up the two seriously injured gunnery ratings, one of which died coming over in the boat. These two, on recovering consciousness, had, in spite of their severe injuries, dragged themselves from under a mess of debris and wreckage, the one dragging himself to the stern where he was observed from the *Sunflower* which had swept close to the wreck. The ship's company of the *Dolius* had looked at the remains of the quarters which were right over the explosion and had considered survival in the mass of debris impossible. It is desired to note here that the conduct and bearing of the ship's company of the *Dolius* from the Master downwards was exemplary throughout. C.Bs were destroyed, a well-ordered discipline was maintained with the Chinese crew. On board *Sunflower* officers and apprentices of the *Dolius* maintained look-out watches; hands assisted to clean quarters with energy, and a lot

of small deck jobs were voluntarily and cheerfully done about the decks. The ship was sorry to see them go in spite of the overcrowding involved. On picking up the survivors (66 out of 70) the *Dolius* was left sinking slowly, and on the Master's opinion a signal was made to *Tay* that the ship was beyond salvage. Course and speed were set to rejoin the convoy. The DEMS rating (AB Stanley Benit, 21) was buried with a short service as the ship rejoined the convoy.

When the forlorn wreck of the *Dolius* had dropped back out of sight, an uneasy silence settled over the convoy. For the first time since leaving the shelter of the North Channel, it seemed that fate was at last dealing ONS 5 a playable hand. The weather was improving by the hour, and the convoy would soon be within range of Canadian air cover based in Newfoundland. Furthermore, the First Support Group, consisting of the sloops *Pelican* and *Sennen* and the frigates *Jed*, *Spey* and *Wear*, had left St John's twenty-four hours earlier and were then steaming at 16 knots to reinforce Sherwood's B 7 escorts. The weather was also about to intervene in their favour as the convoy drew near to the Grand Banks of Newfoundland, notorious for their dense fogs caused by the cold waters of the south-flowing Labrador Current meeting the warm north-going Gulf Stream. However, overshadowing all these favourable factors was the sheer volume of HF/DF bearings being received. Later reports show that in the region of fifteen U-boats, urged on by a stream of signals emanating from Lorient, were circling the convoy like sharks waiting for the opportunity to strike.

First to break through Sherwood's screen was Ralf von Jessen's U-266. Although von Jessen was a comparative newcomer to U-boats, this being only his second war patrol in command, he was no stranger to the whims of the torpedo, having served as Torpedo Officer in the auxiliary cruiser *Thor* during her 329-day cruise in the South Atlantic when she sank or captured nearly 100,000 tons of Allied shipping. Transferring to the U-boat arm in May 1942, von Jessen took command of U-266 on her first venture into the Atlantic and in February 1943 sank the 4,077-ton Greek steamer *Polyktor*. Thereafter, U-266's patrol had been frustratingly disappointing, that is until ONS 5 came over the horizon.

Nervously, anxiously, Ralf von Jessen began a stealthy approach to the convoy's outer port column.

The visibility was good, the sea relatively calm and the tightly packed mass of ships steaming so slowly that at times they appeared to be hove-to. In some ways the scene might be likened to a coconut shy at a fairground, except that there were so many 'coconuts' to chose from that it seemed impossible to miss.

As he neared the outer column, von Jessen lined up his sights on the leading ship and fired a spread of four from his bow tubes. The torpedoes ran neck and neck, their wakes streaming after them as they raced towards the helpless merchantmen. Then the unbelievable happened, and every one of these torpedoes missed, threading their way through the lines of ships as though guided by an unseen hand protecting their targets. They skimmed past ship after ship, sometimes clearing a bow or a stern by only a few feet. Two of the spread eventually passed harmlessly out on to the other side of the convoy to sink unfulfilled, but the others finally struck gold.

At the head of Column 9, the last but one column to starboard, was the 5,136-ton *Selvistan*, owned by Common Brothers of Newcastle, bound from the Tyne to Halifax in ballast. A first cousin to the late *Wentworth*, she had been built by Short Brothers in their Sunderland yard in 1924 and was another typical example of a north-east coast tramp, with a box-shaped hull, tall natural draught funnel and a 363 nhp (nominal horsepower) triple-expansion steam engine that gave her a service speed of 10 knots in fair weather. Between the wars she had worked the charter markets on a 'go anywhere, carry anything' basis, consistently earning good money for her family-owned company. On the outbreak of war in September 1939, the *Selvistan* had been recruited into the transatlantic shuttle along with so many others of her ilk. Four years on, she was a veteran of the North Atlantic convoys, hardened to the habitually bad weather and, so far, seemingly immune to the constant attentions of Dönitz's U-boats.

Commanded by Captain George Miles, the *Selvistan* carried a crew of forty, along with six DEMS gunners. The latter formed the nucleus of the guns' crews who manned her armament of one 4-inch, one 12-pounder and an assortment of machine-guns. Ocean tramp though she might be, the *Selvistan* was a well-found, well-maintained vessel and reputed to be a 'good feeder'. She was a happy ship.

Lulled by the benign weather and the lack of U-boat activity, and in anticipation of the evening meal now on its way from the galley, Captain Miles decided to go below, leaving Chief Officer C. D. Head in charge of the bridge. Perversely, the moment Miles left the bridge things began to happen. In an interview with an Admiralty representative, Chief Officer Head related the events that followed:

> The *Selvistan* was rather close to the next ship abeam, which was an American tanker, when suddenly I saw something moving through the water which at first I thought was a porpoise, as it appeared to be spouting water. This object passed very close across the American tanker's bow, and when it was half way between the *Selvistan* and the American ship, it jumped out of the water and then continued on its course. I immediately realized that it was a torpedo, so I rang 'Full speed ahead' and put the helm hard to port, but unfortunately the ship did not have enough speed to swing clear. This torpedo struck the ship in No. 5 hold on the port side; about five seconds later, we were struck by a second torpedo in No. 4 hold, also on the port side. Both were dull explosions, no flash was seen and no water was thrown up. The hatches and beams from Nos. 4 and 5 holds were blown off, and the ballast from those holds was flung high in the air. The vessel did not list, but settled rapidly by the stern with her bows rising in the air, and within two minutes she was completely submerged.

Chief Officer Head's words – 'unfortunately the ship did not have enough speed to swing clear' – serve to illustrate one of the weaknesses of the convoy system. Whereas sailing in convoy protected by naval escorts was undoubtedly the safest way for the ordinary merchant ship to go to sea in time of war, it also meant that the speed of all in the convoy was restricted to that of the slowest ship. In the case of ONS 5, many of its ships were elderly tramps hard-pressed to work up to 7 or 8 knots, even in an emergency, and the norm was around 6½ knots. Had the

Selvistan been steaming at her customary 10 knots she might well have been able to avoid von Jessen's torpedoes.

With two of her holds blown wide open to the sea, the *Selvistan* went down so quickly that her crew had no time to lower her two lifeboats, although they were swung out ready for launching, as was now standard practice aboard all British merchantmen. They were reduced to abandoning ship in the two small jolly boats carried abreast the bridge and one raft which was launched from the fore deck. In all, forty men left the ship in this way. Chief Officer Head described the evacuation:

> I do not know for certain if either of the lifeboats was damaged, but one of the men told me afterwards that when he was sitting on the raft he saw the port lifeboat break against the davits; he also saw the missing 4th Engineer running towards his boat, but before he could reach it the vessel sank under him.
>
> Gunner Kell, whose skull was smashed in, and Gunner Freeman, who seriously injured his leg, were clinging to a hatch, and as the vessel sank they floated off. I was unable to pick them up as someone had kicked the plug out of my boat and it was filling rapidly, but the 2nd Officer in charge of the port bridge boat rescued them. The Master's raft drifted close to my boat, and as it did so, several sailors jumped out of my boat on to it, leaving me with only the Indian firemen who were simply no use at all; they just sat in the boat, praying to Allah to save them, but not attempting to do anything to save themselves. There were now only 4 men in the port bridge boat, 24 in my starboard bridge boat, and 12 on the Master's raft.

Fortunately for the survivors, they were found by HMS *Tay* within three quarters of an hour and taken on board the frigate. For the injured DEMS gunner, Leading Seaman Kell, help came too late. He died before he could be lifted aboard the frigate. In all, six men died, five of them DEMS gunners who had been standing by the 4-inch gun on the poop when the torpedoes struck directly beneath them. Captain George Miles, Chief Officer Head and thirty-eight other men lived to sail again – and this they would do after a short spell of survivor's leave and a renewal of their sea-going gear. It had become a matter of routine for those who manned the merchant ships, many of whom would suffer multiple torpedoings.

Mindful of their leader's call for action, when darkness approached on the 5th the U-boats moved in on the convoy in force. Conveniently, the wind had dropped to a light breeze, and the visibility was down to 1–2 miles. Conditions were ideal for an attack on the surface.

Anticipating a last throw of the dice by Dönitz, at sunset Lieutenant Commander Sherwood had sent HMS *Sunflower* to sweep ahead with her radar. It was a move that paid an immediate dividend, the corvette picking up a firm echo as soon as she was on station. The echo was small but firm, resembling a surfaced submarine. When *Sunflower* increased speed to investigate, the echo disappeared from the screen, but a few minutes later, the Asdic operator reported a contact close on the port bow. The corvette ran in at full speed, dropping a ten-charge pattern of depth charges as she passed over the target.

As the thunder of the exploding charges faded, *Sunflower*'s radar detected another possible U-boat dead ahead at 3,400yds. Treating this as a new target, which indeed it was, *Sunflower* continued on her course to intercept. Three minutes later, the radar echo had gone, and Asdic reported that a torpedo had been fired.

Forewarned, Lieutenant Commander Plomer altered course to comb the track of the torpedo, and seconds later it passed down the corvette's starboard side. At the same time, a third radar contact was made some 2,000yds to starboard, but Plomer chose to ignore it, continuing in pursuit of the U-boat that had fired the torpedo. Barely two minutes elapsed before the target, a U-boat on the surface, was sighted visually. *Sunflower* immediately opened fire with her 4-inch, but with the third round in the breech the gun jammed.

The gun could not be cleared, so Plomer bore down on the U-boat, hoping to force her under; as he did so, however, his Asdic operator reported that the U-boat they had been pursuing in the first place had fired a full salvo of torpedoes. This was a threat Plomer could not ignore, and in the nick of time he ordered the helm hard over to port and watched as the wake of several torpedoes passed down *Sunflower*'s port side.

This was too close for comfort, and with his 4-inch still out of action, Lieutenant Commander Plomer decided it was time to stop playing cat and mouse with the three U-boats and return to the convoy. *Sunflower* was just coming round on to her new course when Plomer received a message from *Tay* to the effect that *Snowflake* was coming to his aid. At the same time his gunners reported they had cleared the 4-inch and were ready for action again.

Plomer reversed course to re-engage the U-boats, but meanwhile the approaching *Snowflake* had obtained a probable U-boat on her radar and was giving chase. Firing star shell and H.E. alternately, *Snowflake* soon had her U-boat in sight. The enemy boat dived when she saw the corvette bearing down on her, but *Snowflake's* Asdic made contact when she was submerged, and a shower of depth charges exploded around the U-boat while she was still shallow.

What followed was a repeat performance of *Sunflower's* earlier experience. As *Snowflake* ran in to attack, her radar picked up another U-boat on the surface. *Snowflake* was now in real danger, for while she was attacking the first target there was a risk that the second U-boat might weigh in with torpedoes against the corvette. While he was calculating the odds against him, Lieutenant Chesterman kept an eye on the first U-boat with Asdic, at the same time using radar to track the second. When *Snowflake's* radar picked a third echo, again classified as 'U-boat', Chesterman decided that he was taking a risk too far. He broke off the engagement and returned to protect the convoy.

Sunflower, meanwhile, was continuing to take the fight to the enemy. She now had several radar and Asdic contacts and was attacking them enthusiastically, but so far with no apparent result. Then, seeing *Snowflake* returning to the convoy, Plomer decided to follow. In the heat of the moment, and with the visibility now very poor, in altering course to break away, *Sunflower* almost ran *Snowflake* down. While the two corvettes were sorting themselves out, the gathering fog cleared to reveal a U-boat on the surface, heavily damaged and being abandoned by her crew.

At about 0100 on the morning of the 6th, U-125, commanded by Ulrich Folkers, had been located on the surface by HMS *Oribi's* radar. The destroyer had raced in at 20 knots and rammed the U-boat before she was able to dive. U-125, severely damaged and apparently in a sinking condition, had then disappeared into the night, and she was assumed to have sunk. In fact, although she was holed and unable to dive, the U-boat was far from finished. Folkers had radioed Lorient requesting help, and four other boats in the area were ordered to search for her. Three hours later, no help having arrived, U-125 was on the point of sinking, and Folkers had ordered his men to abandon ship when *Snowflake* and *Sunflower* discovered her.

Snowflake was nearer, and Chesterman immediately went in to ram, sheering away at the last minute as five scuttling charges set in U-125's hull exploded. The U-boat now began to founder, leaving her crew of fifty-four struggling in the icy Atlantic.

Lieutenant Chesterman's first instinct was to save lives, and he radioed the Senior Officer Escort in HMS *Tay* requesting permission to pick up the U-boat's crew. The response was, 'Not approved to pick up survivors'. *Snowflake* and *Sunflower* returned to take up station in the convoy escort screen, leaving Ulrich Folkers and his men to die in the night.

Viewed from the safety and comfort of the twenty-first century, it may seem that Lieutenant Commander Sherwood's order to leave the U-boat survivors to die was heartless in the extreme, but it should be remembered that Sherwood and his convoy had been under attack by the U-boats for many days and nights, much of the time in horrendous weather, and with death attendant on every man in every ship, merchant and naval, every hour of every day. Sherwood, not surprisingly, had reached breaking point and was in no mood to be 'magnanimous in defeat'. Too many ships had gone, too many men had died.

It should also be remembered that on 4 May 1943 U-125 had sunk Evan Thomas Radcliffe's *Lorient*, thereby condemning forty-six British merchant seamen to a lonely death. It is said that retribution comes in many forms. Was this one of them?

CHAPTER FOURTEEN

End of the Road

Captain Rodney Stone had been haunting the bridge of the *Gharinda* for so long that he felt as much a part of the fixtures of the wheelhouse as the engine room telegraph he was propped up against. Countless mugs of steaming hot cocoa and plates of dog-eared sandwiches passed up from the pantry had kept him going through the long stressful days and nights, always in fear of the crash of a torpedo against the ship's hull. But now, with journey's end only just over the horizon, perhaps it was time to slacken the reins. Just a little; enough to ease the strain.

As he contemplated relaxing his grip, Stone was completely unaware of U-266's periscope breaking the surface just two columns away to port. It was only when the *Selvistan*, stationed a mere 1,000yds off on the *Gharinda*'s starboard beam, erupted in a cloud of smoke and flame, that he realized there was no such thing as a safe spot in ONS 5 on that unusually fine Atlantic evening.

The 5,306-ton *Gharinda*, owned by the British India Steam Navigation Company and registered in Glasgow, belonged in the past. Built in Sunderland as the First World War was drawing to a bloody close, she had been ordered by the Shipping Controller as a standard replacement ship to be named *War Mavis*. By the time the *War Mavis* was ready to go to sea in 1919 she was surplus to Government requirements and was sold at a knockdown price to the British India, which had lost eighty-five ships in the war. She was renamed *Gharinda* after a small village in the Punjab. Now, at the grand old age of twenty-four, despite careful maintenance over the years, she was long overdue for the breaker's yard and, a little unfairly perhaps, often referred to as 'the wreck of the British India fleet'.

Manned by a complement of ninety-two, made up of seventeen British officers, sixty-five Indian ratings and ten DEMS gunners, in May 1943 the *Gharinda* was far from her usual trading waters in the East, where more often than not blue skies and calm seas prevailed. She had not weathered the storms of the past week very well. Of these, Captain Stone said:

> Bad weather continued, and on the night of the 3rd May, I discovered that we had lost contact with the ship ahead and could not see the Commodore's ship, so I signalled to a destroyer stating, 'I have lost contact with the convoy.' I continued on the course, with two destroyers and two corvettes keeping station on me, proceeding at the convoy speed. At daylight the following day, May 4th, we had completely lost contact with the rest of the convoy, evidently they were being held back by the weather. We turned round and steamed back in the direction from whence we had come at our full speed of 10½ knots; eventually we sighted the convoy trying to get clear of an ice floe. I remained inside the ice until they were clear and at 0900 on the 4th, rejoined the convoy, again taking up my position of No. 111.

Over the following forty-eight hours the weather had undergone a complete change; the ice was far behind them, and the wind had ceased to menace. The *Gharinda*'s log recorded: 'dull, overcast with light rain; visibility fair with a moderate sea and swell, and SW'ly wind, force 3'. After fifteen consecutive days spent in constant conflict with the weather and the U-boats, it is hardly surprising that Captain Stone at last felt he could leave the bridge, to relax, if only for fifteen minutes or so. He later recorded:

> I was having a cup of tea because there hadn't been an alarm for over an hour – I mean, it was as bad as that, if you've got a clear hour it's not too bad going. Normally when you're in command if you get an hour or two hours consecutive sleep you're very lucky. You've got your clothes on all the time; you never take your clothes off. Well I got up on the bridge and a ship on my port beam got it in number-five or number-four hatch and she went down very quickly indeed . . .

The shock of seeing the *Selvistan* disintegrate under the hammer of Ralf von Jessen's torpedoes brought Stone back into the real world, and two minutes later, when the third of von Jessen's spread of four slammed into the *Gharinda's* hull, that world fell apart. Stone's report continues:

> I arrived a moment after it happened but I looked around first to see if anything else might be in the vicinity because that's somebody else's ship, not mine. But having looked round I looked back and saw the captain when he jumped from the bridge into the sea. There was a lifeboat nearby, I knew that. Well, I couldn't stop and pick him up and I suppose it was a matter of half a minute when I got one myself . . .

The torpedo, which had wended its way through the ranks of the convoy, narrowly missing ship after ship, arrived unseen, striking the *Gharinda* on her port side in way of her No. 1 hold. There was a blinding flash, followed by an explosion like a clap of thunder, and the vessel was lifted bodily out of the water. The tarpaulins, hatch boards and beams of the forward hold were blown high in the air, and the debris, accompanied by a column of dirty water, cascaded down on to the bridge. Both the forward derricks, heavy steel booms, were thrown aside and lying at an awkward angle on the hatch tops. Fortunately, the watertight bulkhead between Nos. 1 and 2 holds was not breached, but the *Gharinda* dipped slowly by the head as the empty No. 1 hold filled.

On the bridge, Captain Stone, recovering quickly from the shock of the torpedoing, assessed the situation as critical and hit the alarm button, giving the six short and one long ring signalling 'Abandon Ship!' In the wireless room abaft the bridge, Chief Radio Officer Frank Fox switched on his W/T transmitter and began tapping out a distress on the key. When his signal had been answered by the Commodore's ship *Rena*, Fox shut down his transmitter and ran for the boat deck.

Having given the order to lower the lifeboats, Captain Stone threw his code books over the side in their weighted bags and joined the others on the boat deck.

The *Gharinda* carried six lifeboats, more than sufficient to accommodate her large crew. As the ship did not list, but remained upright, five of these were successfully lowered to the water, but the sixth suffered an all too familiar fate. In the rush to get this boat into the water, the forward fall ran away, and the boat nose-dived into the sea, was swamped and lost. Four of the other boats were clear of the ship within two minutes, however, Captain Stone holding the motor-lifeboat alongside while he searched the ship to ensure that no one was left behind. Modest as ever, he later wrote: ' I did the quickest run around the ship I've ever done in my life to make sure that nobody else was on board, and then I went down the ladder to the lifeboat – I suppose I was about three or four feet above water level.'

Stone's report continues:

> I collected all the boats at a safe distance from the vessel, and transferred all the men with the exception of the 2nd Engineer and 3rd Officer to the other boats. It was my intention to return to the vessel with these two men as she was still afloat; although the propeller and rudder were out of the water, I thought there might be a chance of salving her. Before I could carry out my intentions HMS *Tay* arrived on the scene, and commenced picking, or rather 'hauling' up the survivors. We were literally lifted bodily on board *Tay*, in fact I was hauled up by the scruff of my neck.

Aware that the U-boat that had torpedoed the *Selvistan* and the *Gharinda* was still somewhere in the vicinity, Lieutenant Commander Sherwood was clearly reluctant to waste time on trivialities. Dignity went by the board, and in less than forty minutes all ninety-two of the *Gharinda*'s crew had been taken on board the frigate to join the forty survivors of the *Selvistan* already picked up. Nor was Sherwood receptive to Stone's suggestion that he be allowed to return to his ship, which had still not sunk.

In his report on the torpedoing of his ship, Captain Stone had nothing but praise for the behaviour of his men:

> I would mention that all my officers and the crew, including 68 Indians and 1 Chinaman, behaved extremely well throughout, and happily no-one was injured or lost. This I attribute to the efficient and orderly way the officers and crew carried out their orders. I am extremely pleased with the native crew, because they showed no sign of panic at

any time. I think this is partly due to the fact that on board my ship no English is spoken, all orders are given in the language of the natives, which I consider helps them to understand what is going on, and therefore they are not liable to panic.

In British ships which habitually carried large Indian crews it was customary for the officers to give orders to the ratings, who usually spoke no English, in a crude form of Hindustani known as 'bazaar bat'. The vocabulary of the 'bat' was rather limited, but it was sufficient for the day-to-day running of a ship.

Lieutenant Commander Sherwood commented:

> The crew of the *Gharinda* were all rescued without getting their feet wet. Her captain, a man called Rodney Stone, was sitting in the stern of his boat and I looked down from the wing of the bridge and I could see him sitting there with the biggest gun I've ever seen between his knees. I remember saying something to him about it – I trust it wasn't loaded – but he got it on board and he still has it as far as I know.

Captain Stone's report explains:

> I'd got all my boats in a line, which made it fairly easy for Captain Sherwood on HMS *Tay*, who didn't have to go from one boat to another, all dotted around the place. That was something we were taught – if you get all your boats together and keep together, because if an aeroplane looks for you it's much easier to find a bunch of boats than one solitary boat. I had one of my rifles, which I was very proud of, with me and didn't want to lose it. The only reason I had it was because I'd been cleaning it and I grabbed it as I went down those few steps. Sherwood did ask me if the damned thing was loaded and I said no it wasn't. I was picked up very unceremoniously by the scruff of the neck and thrown on the deck – the same as the rest of my crew and officers – and I went forward to make myself known to Captain Sherwood. My only casualty was the Third Officer who went over the side into the drink – he

sat on the gunwale after I'd told him not to. We pulled him out almost instantly and he couldn't speak, he was so bloody cold. So he was picked up, thrown on the deck and taken straight down to the *Tay's* engine room, otherwise he'd probably have frozen to death. I don't know the temperature of the sea water but I think it was below freezing at the time, because we'd just come out of the ice floes.

The last torpedo of U-266's spread of four to leave its tube was a complete miss, passing right through the columns of ONS 5, narrowly missing ship after ship, ending up in the open water to starboard of the convoy and eventually sinking harmlessly to the bottom. But von Jessen was not finished. He still had a torpedo in his stern tube, and this he fired in the general direction of the ships in Column 8 where, more by good luck than good judgement, it found a target.

Captain Rodney Stone was then performing one of the last rites for the *Gharinda*, the disposal of her secret code books overboard before leaving her, when he was witness to the torpedoing of the small Norwegian ship *Bonde*. This he recorded in his report:

> Just after we were torpedoed, whilst I was on the bridge, about to throw the Confidential Books overboard, I saw the Norwegian ship BONDE open fire with her Oerlikons. Thinking she had sighted the periscope of a submarine, I ordered our Oerlikons to open fire in the direction where the BONDE'S shots were falling. A few seconds later I saw the track of a torpedo approaching the BONDE, and saw the torpedo strike on the starboard side of the vessel.

Stone's observations were confirmed by Captain John Gates of the British steamer *Baron Graham:*

> I saw two ships torpedoed during the daylight hours. One was a small tanker, the *Bonde*. I heard gunfire and turned to see what was happening, and saw the water all along her waterline being whipped into foam. Then there was an explosion and she seemed to jump in the water. When the smoke and spray of the explosion had cleared away,

the *Bonde* was already standing on her end with her bow and foredeck vertically out of the water. I looked away for a few seconds and in that time the ship had sunk.

The *Bonde* was the smallest ship in the convoy at a mere 1,570 tons gross, little more than a coaster. Oslo-registered, she was a fugitive from the German occupation of Norway, whence she fled in 1940, eventually coming under the control of the British Ministry of War Transport. Built in Norway in 1936, in pre-war days she had rarely ventured beyond the relatively sheltered waters of the Baltic or North Sea, but that was now a thing of the past, and Britain's needs were great. Under charter to J. E. Murell & Son of West Hartlepool, the *Bonde* was carrying nearly 2,000 tons of anthracite, loaded in the Bristol Channel, and was facing up to the perils of the North Atlantic shoulder to shoulder with her big sisters. Chief Officer M. Macellan of the *Baron Graham* had this to say of her:

> *Bonde* was the little ship we all admired so much in that convoy. In such a vast expanse of sea she looked so tiny as she courageously battled through the heavy seas and swells. The first thing I used to do as daylight broke in my morning watch was to look for our little friend, and if she was bobbing along the day was made.

Sailing under the command of Captain Finn Abrahamsen, the *Bonde* carried a total complement of twenty-six, of which her radio officer, one able seaman, the messboy and five DEMS gunners were British, a common enough mix at this stage of the war. She was powered by a 2-cylinder compound steam engine with a nominal horse power of only 68, which nevertheless gave her a top speed of 10 knots.

The first indication Captain Abrahamsen had of the impending danger came when the DEMS gunners manning the *Bonde*'s after gun platform spotted a periscope some 400yds off on the starboard beam. They immediately opened fire on it with the 20mm Oerlikon, but were too late to spoil Kapitänleutnant von Jessen's aim. His torpedo caught the *Bonde* right aft on her starboard side, literally blowing her stern clean off. The after watertight bulkhead of the engine room collapsed, and the sea poured into the engine room and stokehold. Her propeller and rudder gone, and her engines disabled, the Norwegian ship was in her death throes.

With the *Bonde* settling by the stern at an alarming rate, Captain Abrahamsen ordered his crew to take to the boats. Those who had been unfortunate enough to be in the engine room and after part of the vessel when the torpedo struck were already dead, and only ten men answered Abrahamsen's call to launch the boats. The doomed ship, now stopped and beam-on to the wind and sea, had developed a dangerous roll, and it was only with great difficulty that one lifeboat and one liferaft were lowered to the water. The eleven survivors boarded, pulled clear of the ship, and stood off to watch her go under, but the *Bonde*, being a well-found little ship, refused to sink. An hour later, when HMS *Tay* came to rescue her survivors, she was still afloat.

Once aboard the frigate, Captain Abrahamsen persuaded Lieutenant Commander Sherwood to allow him to return to his ship to assess her chances of survival. Abrahamsen, First Mate Rasmus Rasmussen, Second Mate Edvard Jensen, Radio Officer Vincent Willox and two Able Seamen then took the lifeboat back to the *Bonde* and re-boarded her. A quick inspection of the ship revealed that she was beyond saving, but the persistence of Captain Finn Abrahamsen was rewarded by the discovery of another survivor, Second Engineer Nils Pettersen, who had escaped from the flooded engine room alive.

Captain Abrahamsen's description of the end of his ship is at odds with accounts given by eyewitnesses in other ships, who all stated that they saw her sink within a matter of minutes. The Purser of the British motor vessel *Losada*, at the head of Column 5, said, 'It was really incredible. We watched, glued to where we stood, with our mouths wide open. I, for one, had not realized that a ship could sink so quickly. In a couple of minutes – I am sure it was no more – her bows and stern were out of the water, and then she was gone.' It could be that this account was influenced by the drama of the moment, but the *Losada*'s Purser was only one of several who remarked on the speed of the *Bonde*'s demise, whereas Captain Abrahamsen and his men were obviously aboard the ship for some time. The only plausible explanation for this apparent contradiction lies with the visibility, which was then falling, the convoy entering a fog bank shortly afterwards.

The loss of three ships in as many minutes, and in broad daylight, sent a heavy shock wave running through the ranks of ONS 5. Lieutenant Mike Downes, *Tay's* navigator recalled:

I clearly remember being on afternoon watch on 5 May looking around towards the convoy in time to see three ships hit almost simultaneously. The first was *Selvistan*, which sank stern first. *Gharinda* sank bow first and the little ship *Bonde* broke in two. All three sank within two minutes. It was a sight I'll never forget. These were the last of our ships sunk and at this point the score was 11 ships to one U-boat. We had a rescue ship, the trawler *Northern Spray*, which was full, having picked up 146 survivors. *Tay* picked up some 143 other survivors from those three ships and this also made us very crowded as our own crew was only 126.

Commodore Brook reacted quickly to the attack, signalling for a 90° emergency turn to port which, surprisingly enough, was executed without undue confusion, while Lieutenant Commander Sherwood sent his escorts racing around the convoy with their Asdics pinging. At 1830, with the sun low on the horizon, HMS *Oribi* gained a firm underwater contact, and over the next hour and a half she pursued the echo, dropping five 10-charge patterns. She then lost contact, and it was wrongly assumed that the U-boat had been sunk. In fact, the target of Lieutenant Commander Ingram's depth charges, which was later identified as Ralf von Jessen's U-266, had escaped, but not without considerable damage. When he was clear of the area, von Jessen reported to BdU that one of his diving tanks and several trim cells were damaged, while his air compressor and starboard dynamotor were out of action, but onboard repairs were possible. He was ordered to withdraw to quieter waters.

Seventy-two hours later, her repairs completed, U-266 was ordered to join other boats which were assembling for a pack attack on the eastbound convoy SC 129, then on its way from Halifax to Liverpool. Consisting of twenty-five loaded merchantmen escorted by two destroyers, five corvettes and two armed trawlers, SC 129 had been the subject of much intelligence activity since sailing. Having broken the British convoy code, German Intelligence had discovered the route of the convoy, and Dönitz was preparing an ambush. Not to be outdone, Bletchley Park had likewise penetrated the U-boat code, and SC 129 was re-routed around the waiting pack. However, unknown to the Admiralty, by then the Germans had discovered the new route and had moved their ambush to cover it.

When SC 129, now diverted to a more southerly route, reached a position 150 miles north-west of the Azores, it was set upon by another pack of thirty U-boats, including U-266, which had returned to the fray. The convoy's escorts put up a spirited defence, the battle ranging over many miles of ocean and lasting for some three days, but SC 129's escorts, although now tired and nearing the end of their ammunition, held the attackers at bay.

On the night of 14 May, while manoeuvring to attack, U-266 was caught on the surface by a Halifax of No. 58 Squadron RAF, piloted by Wing Commander W. E. Oulton. The aircraft carried the first Mark 24 mine to be used operationally, a homing torpedo activated by propeller noise. True to form, the torpedo homed in on U-266's propellers, and Ralf von Jessen and his crew of forty-six all died with their boat. SC 129 reached Liverpool a week later, having lost two merchantmen in return for two U-boats sunk.

Returning to ONS 5, as darkness approached on the 5th, the convoy, making a rapid recovery after the sudden mauling it had received at the hands of Ralf von Jessen, had re-formed into twenty-three ships in ten columns abreast and was on a course of 202° at 6½ knots. The corvette *Pink* was following behind with her four stragglers. HF/DF was still picking up a great deal of German radio traffic around the convoy, indicating that the U-boats were still out there, circling like a pack of hungry wolves. This was substantiated by a signal from the Admiralty which read, '25 U-boats in contact with your convoy, 40 in the immediate vicinity closing, 70 in general area'. Later reports showed that at least fifteen boats were then in close proximity to the convoy and that Dönitz was urging them to deliver the coup de grâce to ONS 5 before reinforcements arrived from St John's.

In anticipation of another busy night, Lieutenant Commander Sherwood arranged his escort screen accordingly. *Tay* was scouting ahead, *Sunflower* on the port bow, *Vidette* on the starboard bow, *Snowflake* on the port quarter and *Loosestrife* on the starboard quarter. Five miles out on either bow were the destroyers *Offa* and *Oribi*. Soon after the screen was in place, *Tay* sighted seven U-boats ahead in the gathering dusk. At about the same time, Günter Gretschel in U-707 reported to BdU, 'I am positioned within sight of seven boats, in front of the convoy.' He later said, 'I wanted to make a joint attack in the darkness. Unfortunately, the weather had thwarted our plans. The visibility has gotten very bad, with fog and drizzle, and this makes any attack impossible in the pitch-black night.'

The onset of darkness and the deteriorating visibility were all to Sherwood's advantage. And the mixture of drizzle and mist was only a precursor of what was to come. ONS 5 was moving into the fog-bound waters of the Grand Banks of Newfoundland, and the B 7 escorts were all equipped with the new Type 271M radar. While this was a primitive instrument compared with modern radar, having a small cathode ray tube and a hand-trained aerial which gave only a bearing and range of an echo, it could not be detected by the U-boats' Metox sets, thereby putting the Germans at a great disadvantage in fog.

U-531, a long-range Type IXC/40 under the command of Kapitänleutnant Herbert Neckel, was first to fall to Sherwood's radar. Commissioned at Hamburg in October 1942, U-531 was on her first war patrol and had experienced a run of bad luck since sailing from Kiel on 13 April. Nine days into the Atlantic, while passing between Iceland and the Faroe Islands, she was attacked by a Catalina of 120 Squadron RAF, and again later in the day by a B-27 Flying Fortress of 206 Squadron. On both occasions U-531 escaped unharmed, but this early baptism of fire did not improve the morale of her crew.

U-531 had arrived in the vicinity of ONS 5 at the end of April, but it was not until early evening on 5 May that Neckel saw the opportunity to contribute to the attack on the convoy and, perhaps, to send his first enemy ship to the bottom. Taking advantage of the restricted visibility, he remained on the surface and moved closer to the convoy, approaching on the starboard bow. The first likely target to come into sight was the leading ship of ONS 5's Column 12, the 4,272-ton British steamer *Empire Planet*. In ballast, like so many others in the convoy, riding high out of the water and making a leisurely 6½ knots on a straight course, she offered an easy shot.

But Herbert Neckel was denied the pleasure of sinking his first enemy ship. As he lined up his sights in the conning tower, U-531 showed up on HMS *Vidette*'s radar. *Vidette*, an Admiralty 'V' class destroyer of First World War vintage, was not a fast mover, but when U-531 emerged from the mist only 700yds ahead of her, Lieutenant Commander Hart called for emergency full speed, and she positively leapt forward. At the same time he ordered the forward 4-inch to open fire, but in the excitement of the moment the gun's crew fired with only the cordite charge in the breech. The result was a loud bang and a blinding flash, which led those on the destroyer's bridge to believe they had been hit.

The flash also alerted Herbert Neckel to the approaching danger, and he immediately cleared the conning tower and took U-531 down in a crash-dive. She was only just below the surface when *Vidette* ran over her, releasing a l0-charge pattern of depth charges.

U-531 failed to return to her Biscay base and was never heard of again. It was assumed that Herbert Neckel and his crew of fifty-three had perished as a result of HMS *Vidette*'s depth charges.

Daylight on 6 May saw the arrival from St John's of the 1st Escort Support group led by Commander Geoffrey Brewer in the sloop HMS *Pelican*, with the River-class frigates *Jed*, *Spey* and *Wear* and the ex-US Coastguard cutter HMS *Sennen*. These ships, fully ammunitioned and with their crews rested and eager to join the fight, were enough to turn the tables on the U-boats. The Germans were fully aware of the changing situation, as illustrated by BdU's War Diary for the day:

> The operation against the convoy was broken off at 0600 for the following reasons: from 0400 in AJ 8562 there was no further contact with the convoy. The thick fog made it extremely unlikely that the convoy would be found again. In places visibility was only 200 metres and the danger kept increasing of the boats being surprised by locating destroyers, in fact several boats reported this. U 125 reported that she had been rammed in the stern by a destroyer, and almost all the boats were depth charged, as the convoy escort were easily able to find the boats by location. There was no prospect of the weather improving, as the convoy was approaching the Newfoundland Bank.

For ONS 5 it had been a long and exhausting battle against the most fearful odds, a battle fought not only against the massed ranks of Dönitz's U-boats, but also against the cruel North Atlantic weather. Despite the unflagging efforts of Escort Group B-7, thirteen ships had been lost and 114 men had died, but at long last the U-boats had been given a bloody nose, a victory confirmed by a communiqué issued by BdU:

> The boats had a bad time. Merely, during this period, 15 boats were depth charged, and six of these were suddenly attacked with gunfire by locating destroyers. As they had no counter measures against location, the boats were definitely at a disadvantage and had little prospect of success. In all, 4 boats were so badly damaged that they had to give up the attack. U 125 did not report again after she had been rammed, nor was she found by the 4 boats that searched for her. Besides this boat 5 more did not report: U 638, U 438, U 531, U 630 and U 192. Three of these boats had reported contact with the enemy convoy.
>
> If none of these boats report later, this loss of six boats is very high and grave considering the short duration of the attack.

Official figures issued by the Admiralty at a later date show six U-boats sunk by the convoy's escorts and two by aircraft. In addition, seven boats were so badly damaged that they had to withdraw from the action, while eleven others received minor damage. A total of 364 U-boat crewmen lost their lives.

ONS 5 arrived in Halifax, NS on 12 May. From there the merchantmen dispersed to their various loading ports to take on cargoes for the return passage. All too soon they would then face the prospect of reliving the nightmare from which they had just emerged. The unending battle against the cruel winter weather would continue, while all the time they would have to watch and wait for the crash of an enemy torpedo slamming against their hull, condemning them to the grip of the icy Atlantic. There was no rest for Escort Group B-7 either. In a few days they were back at sea challenging the Atlantic with an eastbound convoy.

Epilogue

Black May 1943 marked the end of the domination of the North Atlantic sea lanes by the U-boats. The debacle of ONS 5 was followed two weeks later by the humiliation of Convoy SC 130, in which Dönitz sent a wolf pack of twenty-five U-boats against thirty-seven merchantmen escorted by Commander Peter Gretton's B-7 Group. In a fiercely fought running battle the U-boats failed to sink or damage a single ship, losing three of their number in the process.

Close in the wake of SC 130 came HX 239, a convoy of forty-two ships which sailed from New York on 13 May. Forewarned by B-Dienst, Dönitz set up an ambush, but in spite of the large number of U-boats involved, the convoy came through intact. In this case, the presence of the escort carrier HMS *Archer*, which gave continuous air cover to the convoy, was the deciding factor. Dönitz lost two more of his steadily dwindling band of U-boats, and again no Allied ship was sunk.

In his memoir *Ten Years and Twenty Days*, published in 1958, Karl Dönitz wrote:

> The overwhelming superiority achieved by the enemy defence was finally proved beyond dispute in the operations against the next two convoys SC 130 and HX 239. The convoy escorts worked in exemplary harmony with the specially trained support groups.
>
> To that must be added the continuous air cover, which was provided by carrier-borne and long-range shore-based aircraft, most of them equipped with the new radar. There were also new and heavier depth charges and improved means of throwing them. With all this against us it became impossible to carry on the fight.

On 24 May 1943, Admiral Dönitz, then quietly mourning the loss of his youngest son Peter, who had gone down with U-954 in the abortive attack on SC 130, finally admitted defeat and withdrew his wolf packs from the North Atlantic convoy lanes. He gave the new centimetric radar carried by most Allied escort vessels and aircraft as the primary reason for his defeat, claiming:

> Radar, and particularly radio location by aircraft, had to all practical purposes robbed the U-boats of their power to fight on the surface. Wolf-pack operations against convoys in the North Atlantic, the theatre of operations and at the same time the theatre in which air cover was strongest, were no longer possible.

There can be little doubt that Allied radar, particularly the British Type 271, which the Metox sets carried by the U-boats could not detect, did play a very significant part in their defeat, but there were other factors.

At that time, American and Canadian shipyards, using pre-fabrication, were turning out replacement merchant ships at an unprecedented rate. A 7,000-ton American Liberty ship, for instance, could be assembled and launched in just forty days, and two of these Libertys were coming down the slipway every twenty-four hours. This must have been soul-destroying for the U-boat men, who at the height of the battle in late 1942 were sinking ships faster than the Allies could build them.

In four years of war the progress of Allied technology had been phenomenal, but Karl Dönitz would have been the first to admit that, in the end, his U-boats were defeated by the sheer professionalism and tenacity of the British and Canadian escort ships, the destroyers, sloops, frigates and corvettes. And then there was the quiet stoicism of the men of the merchant ships who, in the face of a deliberate campaign to wipe them from the face of this earth, held fast. Seafaring down the ages has always been a hazardous occupation, but overnight the sea had become a killing ground in which one man in every three was losing his life to the enemy's guns and torpedoes. Yet they still kept coming back, voyage after voyage, after voyage . . . They were the rock on which Dönitz's dreamboat eventually foundered.

Bibliography

Books

Blair, Clay, *Hitler's U-boat War 1939–1942*, Cassell & Co., 2000

Carruthers, Bob, *The U-boat War in the Atlantic, 1942–1943*, Pen & Sword, 2013

Course, Captain A. G., *The Deep Sea Tramp*, Hollis & Carter, 1960

Divine, A. D., *The Merchant Navy Fights*, John Murray, 1940

Dönitz, Karl, *Ten Years and Twenty Days*, Naval Institute Press, 1990

Gannon, Michael, *Black May*, Arum Press, 1998

Gretton, Sir Peter, *Convoy Escort Commander*, Cassell & Co., 1964

Jones, Geoffrey, *Defeat of the Wolf Packs*, William Kimber, 1986

Middlebrook, Martin, *Convoy*, William Morrow, 1976

Morgan, Daniel and Bruce Taylor, *U-boat Attack Logs*, Seaforth Publishing, 2011

Padfield, Peter, *Dönitz: The Last Führer*, Cassell & Co., 2001

Preston, Anthony, *The Navies of World War II*, Bison Books, 1979

Rohwer, Jurgen, *Axis Submarine Successes of World War Two*, Greenhill Books, 1998

Showell, J. P. Mallmann, *U-boats under the Swastika*, Ian Allan, 1973

Slader, John, *The Fourth Service*, Robert Hale, 1994

Terraine, John, *Business in Great Waters*, Leo Cooper, 1989

Thomas, David A., *The Atlantic Star*, W. H. Allen, 1990

Werner, Herbert A., *Iron Coffins*, Cassell & Co., 1969

Woodman, Richard, *The Real Cruel Sea*, John Murray, 2004

Other Sources

The National Archives

U-boat Net

U-boat Archive

Index